HIGH —on— LIFE

SUE A. MCLAUGHLIN

iUniverse®

HIGH ON LIFE

iUniverse books may be ordered through booksellers or by contacting:

iUniverse
1663 Liberty Drive
Bloomington, IN 47403
www.iuniverse.com
1-800-Authors (1-800-288-4677)

ISBN: 978-1-4917-9651-1 (sc)
ISBN: 978-1-4917-9652-8 (e)

Print information available on the last page.

iUniverse rev. date: 04/29/2016

Contents

High on Life

My pulses race, my eyes are sparkling bright,
My heart flutters within my breast—
Oh my…..I'm high…..on life!

The sun shines brightly, it's warmth so comforting,
The rain falls gently, cooling down the land—
It feels good to be…..high on life!

It wasn't always this way, but that's another day and time,
And I'm never going back to the way it was—
I'm grateful that…..I'm high on life!

Even in the valleys there's a joy within my heart,
And praises on my lips when days are gray—
I still am …..high on life!

The excitement's ever building to magnificent crescendo.
I hear the music everywhere surrounding me—
I'm really high …..I'm high on life!

PENSIVE POETRY

Care-Full Woman

Sadness settled gently on her shoulders,
Sorrow seemed to be so fitting there.
Worry was imprinted on her forehead
As she quietly made room for one more care.

A line for every tear she'd ever shed.
Every tragedy in life was there reflected
In every silver hair upon her head—
But then she smiled!

I Did

Twenty years from the day I was born
I looked and thought, "I could have".

At thirty years I awoke one morn
And said to myself, "I would have".

Forty years it took me to form
All the reasons I should have.

Lord, please let me awake
The last day of my life

And look back and say.......... "I DID"!

Cloudy Sunset

Silvered pewter clouds above a polished pewter sea,
But, lo, a glint of gold there to the west!
Putty-colored sand amid the rivulets of water,
Tinted lightly where the sun caressed.

Breezes moving swiftly in the evening's waning light,
Scuttling waves and clouds before their paths;
Rippling steel gray waves dappled by the gold,
Seabirds tiptoe lightly down for their nocturnal baths.

The undulating seashore of beige and taupe and tan
Seems to be anticipating night.
The heavens wait with bated breath the climax of the day
When the golden sun extinguishes its light.

Even in a cloudy sky the glory of the sunset
Manifests itself in full array;
As with one final burst of splendor the sun-flame is extinguished
And dusky evening settles down to stay.

I Am an Anchor

I am an anchor in a turbulent sea,
I am a harbor sheltered from the elements;
Friend and acquaintance can rely on me.
I am a rock on which one may lean,
A resting place that's warm and secure
Against all dangers seen and unseen.

I am *no* anchor, but a vacillating weed
Bobbing and weaving on that frothing sea,
Searching for an anchor to cling to in *my* need.
Where are all those who leaned on me
When I want to lean, in *my* weariness,
And feel safe and secure from that tumultuous sea?

But, I am and anchor! I have to be—
For that is my excuse for existence.

Trees

I think that I shall never see—
No, Kilmer already did that, splendidly.
But I can still be in awe of a tree
And how they have affected me.
They stand so tall and so stately,
And often provide their shade for me.
There are those whose fruit I eat gladly
And those of such magnificent beauty
That one must just gaze appreciatively,
Caught up in poignant enormity
Of one of God's blessings, created for me!
No, this poem can never do justice to a tree—
Neither did Kilmer's, if you ask me!

Dawn

Slowly and surely comes the dawn,
As the sun peeps o'er the hill,
Coming after the night has gone
When everything is still.

To begin the new day with perfection
And steal away the night.
Without suspicion of detection,
That everyone may deem if right.

Deep Blue World

There's a strange unearthly music
  To the silence of the sea:
Diving down beneath the waters,
  Deep as any man can be.
Colors only once before encountered
  In the corners of your mind;
Things you've never once imagined.
  In that deep blue world you'll find
Coral fingers outward-reaching,
  Grasping for eternity;
Down to basics—living, struggling,
  Basis for humanity.
    A fish in a fish in a fish in a fish,
      Color on color on color on color,
        Moving, lurching, seeking, searching,
        Deep,
          Deep,
            Down.

Happiness

Can happiness be measured?
Can anybody know
Of all the dreams you've treasured
And just what makes them so?
Can it be measured in degrees,
Or ounce or ton or pound?
Can they say that you are happy
Or tell you when you're blue?
Who are they to say you should be,
How can they tell you what to do?
Don't they know you can act happy
When your heart has broken in two?
Can they say you really should be
When there's nothing left for you?
They say to think that you are happy
And the thought will make it so,
But they can't show you how to be
When they don't really know.
If you've never really had it,
If you've never really known,
What can you do to find it,
And how can you be shown?
And if someday you find it,
And happiness comes to you,
Can you be sure to keep it—
Do you know what to do?
Are you going to let it slip away
And do not a thing to stop it,
Or work and strive to make it stay
And do your best to top it.

Leave Your Watch At Home

Leave your watch at home, my friend,
And see how close you come
To forgetting time.
    You won't.

Your body tells you when to eat
Or when it's time to sleep
Or roll over in the sun.
    You'll know.

Leave your watch at home, and then
You'll soon be looking at the sun
Or moon or stars.
    You will.

You want to see how close you come;
Time doesn't really mean a thing—
You can forget it.
    You can't.

Leave your watch at home sometime;
You needn't be a slave to time,
But time can also be a friend.
    So let it.

Fortunate One

Across the room and through the glass doors
I'm gazing at the wondrous scene before me;
Watching the trees and bushes undulating,
Sitting at my table with my second cup of tea.

How can I ever leave this pastoral panorama?
I am such a fortunate one!

Then I recall lying near another window,
Prostrate upon my cushions near the windowsill
I viewed the magnificent oak tree near at hand
Close enough to touch, but I am still.

How can I ever leave this peaceful scene?
I am such a fortunate one!

On the sandy, sun-kissed golden beach,
Awash with mixed emotions, I recline;
Gazing at the sparkling, dancing waters,
Watching the cloudless sky, I lie supine.

How can I ever leave this memorable montage?
I am such a fortunate one!

But I know I'll find other scenes as sweet
Because I am such a fortunate one.

Conclusion

Many happy hours have I spent—
  Those bright days,
    Those happy days.
Many lovely Springs came and went—
  Such glad days,
    Some sad days.

And now that they are gone I feel
  That half my life is through;
    Feelings of sadness o'er me steal,
My heart is sad and blue;
  This is the end of the beginning,
    This is the beginning of the end,
      This is the Conclusion.

Were these my last few day on earth
  Oh, bright earth,
    Oh, beautiful earth.
I could not know more of its worth,
  The great worth,
    Oh bounteous earth.

Were this my last I could not entertain
  More wonder of expectation;
    But were this my last I could hope in vain
For the magnificent revelation.
  This is but the ending of my youth
    This is the end of youthful joy and life;
      This is the Conclusion.

The happy faces that have surrounded me—
  Gay youth,
    Carefree youth.
Enjoying life so full and abundantly—
  Youthful life,
    Free from strife.

No more will I see them smile again
  Or talk and walk and laugh with me;
    And if we ever meet again
We all will have changed so completely!
  I mourn for my lost youth
    For the life that is past,
      This is the Conclusion.

The Librarian

Hundreds and hundreds of books there are
Awaiting my earnest inspection,
Trying to label and categorize
Ascertaining my minute detection.
I ask myself if it's good, bad or indifferent,
Trying not to be the sole arbiter of taste;
Just necessarily weeding out some of them
That I deem would be a huge waste.

I catch myself racing to get through them all,
Reading most at a rapid pace,
While realizing that I cannot keep them all—
We simply do not have the space.
Many I enjoy—a really good read!
Some I just cannot put down.
I feel committed to finish a series I've started
By an author of world-wide renown.

Then some, I can tell you, are not worth the paper
And ink they are printed upon.
(I realize, of course, that it's just one man's opinion)
Some are significant and some are just fun.
The big ones, the small ones and those in between,
I love reading them, or just lightly perusing.
Hardbound or paperback, they all have their place,
There's an infinite assortment for choosing.

I love rearranging and sorting the volumes
To make better use of the space.
I especially enjoy inventorying them all—
Title and author—a complete database.
Yes, it's a big job, but not if you love it.
There are times when it seems mind-bending;
I get great ideas for my own "works of art",
But I know that the task is ne'er-ending.

Different

This is the strangest sensation. I just don't feel like me;
A little light-headed, a little distraught, just not what I want to be.
Is it something I will get over soon—that which will go away,
Or a feeling I'll have to get used to and live with day after day?
A little weak, a bit fragile, just not the "me" that I know.
Should I take a pill for something, or simply lie down for a while?
Baby myself or push myself and force myself to smile?
It's the strangest sort of sensation—not good, not bad,
Nor indifferent; Guess I'll have to reconcile that
From now on I'll just feel......different.

He

HE is strong and manly and omnipotent,
But I don't *feel* like universal.
I don't feel like HE.
I have trouble being me.

HE, in caps, denotes the divine deity.
But I don't feel divine;
I want what's mine,
And sometimes more.

Am I either gender?
Macho, Tuffo, Male,
Sweet, Sensitive, Gentleman?
Or something in between?

Maybe all of the above—and more.
I am He—the universal pronoun.
But this man is not the universal man,
Simply......ME.

Excitement Within

I feel an excitement building within me,
I am not sure just yet what the meaning will be;
I just feel like a little girl swinging in a big tree:
An indescribable feeling of being free!

I'm finished with doldrums and pity party,
Instead I intend to be found laughing hearty!
I'll no more be seen as an object of charity;
Once more I'll be full of jocularity.

Something's coming, something profound!
There's a fresh wind a-blowing and joy in the very ground.
There's an air of exhilaration all around
And an aura of happiness seems to abound.

Again I will leap once more into the fray,
To begin living life for another day;
To love and to laugh, to dance and to play,
Tho' I know that my fears I will never allay.

There's a well of anticipation bubbling in me,
Threatening to burst forth momentarily,
When the excitement culminates, breaking free,
I believe I may fly away—indubitably!

Midnight

Hark! The clock is striking twelve.
    It's Midnight.
The day has turned to night.

I hear the clock on the shelf
    Strike Midnight.
Soon 'twill again be light.

It's that bewitching hour
    Of Midnight,
When everyone's asleep.

The night is so very still
    At Midnight,
As around the corner I creep.

The house is so empty
    At Midnight.
Silence everywhere.

If I could only see
    The Midnight
Floating on the air.

But, alas, my reverie is done,
    For Midnight
Is o'er and I'll soon see the sun.

Memories

We're all part and parcel of our memories—
Part of our brain and sinew and bone.
The good, the bad, the trite and terrific,
The times we feel we're so terribly alone.
Groups and couples and families,
Those present and those long gone.
Recriminations, regrets, remorse,
Projects completed and those undone.
All are part of who we were
And who we have become.
Embrace them all for what they are:
Without them all we are. . . no one.

Life Is But a Dream

Life is but a dream,
A wonderful, lovely dream;
Life is only a scheme,
A complicated scheme.

But alas! It ends too soon,
And the beautiful night sublime—
The sun, the stars, the moon
Are but a fragment of time.

Life is but a dream,
The smallest fraction of time;
Perhaps unkind it will seem,
To some worth nary a dime.

Yes, perhaps life is hard,
Perhaps, at times, dull and dreary;
But lest time should be marred,
Be joyful, though you be weary.

Life is but a dream and
It ends far too soon for me.
We'll soon be heading for dreamland,
Sailing over that heavenly sea.

The moon and stars above us,
The land and the sea below,
Ne'er lacking for someone to love us,
For He is there, we know.

Lifeguard

The beach is lonely and deserted now;
No more crowds and excitement and joy,
No more children playing in the sand,
No more lone, lost lifeguard boy.

The sun is dying, just as he did,
Gone to another (better?) place.
How can such a short span of time
End a life with such erase?

The beach, once my favorite place,
Now lonely, deserted and stark.
It seems fitting, somehow, that no one's there now
As the day approaches the dark.

God must have a plan for the one
The lifeguard gave his life to save.
There's a special place in heaven
For those who are so brave.

An old life saved, while a young one
Was snuffed out in the blink of an eye—
In a matter of minutes it was—
Who can know the answer to "why"?

Never

Never is such a lonely word—
Not to see a loved one anymore;
Never is sometimes a frustrating word,
As in never to do something again;
It can be an extremely sad word
If you can no longer accomplish something, but then
It is also a very hopeful word:
To never have to be or do that which you hate
Ever, ever, and ever! Amen!

Reason vs Desire

Desire is my constant companion
I cannot but be consumed with its lure;
Ever asserting its hold over me,
Its power is controlling and sure.
My longing for what I cannot have,
The yearning for that which I'll never possess
Is controlling my thoughts, my very life—
How it's affecting me I can only guess!

I need to know what my life is about—
How much is real and good and true;
When is longing an acceptable aspiration,
And when is it that which I should rue?
When does a desire become so all-consuming
That nothing on earth that I can gauge
Fulfills that yearning, that craving, that need
That only the object of my desire can assuage?

Then, finally, Reason at last o'ertakes my soul,
Silently, swiftly, with no discernible changing,
My life and my thoughts are metamorphosed.
Common Sense and Desire are there, exchanging.
Reason does not come in to replace Desire,
But more to level it out and explain its might;
To rationalize the one with the other
And show that reasoning can make it all right.

Ah, Reason, sweet Reason, you're welcome
To come into my life and enhance it.
To even thwart Desire, if need be,

Or go on to fruition—to chance it!
Now I know Desire is not my enemy,
But the way I've given it complete control,
I had failed to assign them both proper place,
Had failed to allow Reason its role.

Little Things

A little girl in pigtails, skipping down the road;
Little boys with marbles a baseball or a toad;
An old man trudging homeward, stumbling with his load.

Tiny tots in rompers, playing with their toys,
The bully of the neighborhood teasing little boys,
Women screaming shrilly, "Don't make so much noise!"

Couples in the Chapel, promising "I will",
Trees rustling in the daytime and at night when all is still,
Lilies floating on the lake, the church upon the hill.

The twinkling stars, the sun, the ships upon the sea,
A set of jacks, a little ball, a book of poetry,
These are the little things that mean so much to me.

Panoramic View

I'm perched atop my mountain,
Surveying my kingdom below;
I am viewing the panorama
God has chosen to bestow:

The greens and grays and beiges
And all the colors in between:
Blues of sky and browns of earth—
All His creation can be seen.

It looks like a gigantic canvas,
A magnificent tapestry loom,
This splendid sight I am envisioning
From the window of my room.

People

People are funny or pretty or nice,
Ugly or mean or sweet;
Some are untidy or skinny or tall,
Others are short, fat or neat.

Some like to read in a cozy chair,
Or walk down the road in the rain;
Some yearn for the thrill of a gangster's lair,
Or romance to be theirs again.

But no matter how they look or speak,
And what they say or do,
And whether they be strong or weak,
They're people, just like me and you.

Perfect Seashell

A walk along the seashore
May be good for more than that—
A timely lesson it may teach.

If you really listen to the
Soothing voices of the waves
A simple message they will preach.

Running, scurrying, seeking, sometimes finding,
Looking for that special seashell on the beach;
Bending, stooping, peering, grabbing for that one
There—just out of reach.

Then, stop, lay supine upon the shore—relax!
Contemplate the beauty of the seagull tracks,
Stretch out upon the warm, inviting sand,
Then open up your eyes—there by your hand—
That tiny, elusive, lovely, perfect shell!

Realism vs Idealism

Look upon his countenance—
  Somber, immobile,
    Seldom smiling, seldom frowning;
He never gazes into space—daydreaming;
  Never dreaming, never scheming,
    Save when a practical need arises.
      He is a Realist.

Look upon his countenance—
  Smiling, expectant,
    Apprehensive, fearful,
Gazing into space—daydreaming.
  Always scheming,
    For no reason at all,
      He is an Idealist.

Will you go through life
  Thinking everything through
    Thinking practically
      Taking things as they come
Not dreaming of the future,
  Not seeing the beauty in everything,
    Not seeing the good in everyone,
      Believing solely in predestination.
        Will you be only a Realist?

Will you go through life
  Thinking impractically,
    Not accepting things as they come,
Dreaming of the future,
  Seeing beauty in everything
    Seeing the good in everyone,
Believing, not necessarily in
  Predestination, but
    Always in Life?
      Will you be strictly an Idealist?

A well-balanced individual
    Should deal in Realism.
A well-balanced individual
    Should also be an Idealist.

She

She waits for her lover to come, when he decides,
And he'll come, eventually, if love abides.
She waits for a husband to come home at day's end—
If his work is done and nothing better beckons around the bend.

She waits for the telephone to ring—a human voice—
A conversation with one she wouldn't have called by choice.
She waits through an anxious evening, trying not to overreact,
For a teenage son to come home, with him, and the car, intact.

She waits and worries and fears, at the moment of birth.
"She" is a lonely pronoun—the loneliest on earth.

Alone

When I'm all by myself...............I'm alone.
When I cry................I cry alone.
When I laugh.............I laugh alone.
When I hear something great..........I repeat it alone.
When there is a crisis..............I face it alone.
When I need prayer.............I pray alone.
When I need encouragement...............I encourage myself.
When I go shopping.............I shop alone.
When I read.................I read alone
When I enjoy hobbies...........I enjoy them alone.
When special thoughts come............I treasure them alone.
When I write............I write alone.
I entered this world alone.
I will exit this world alone.
But at my final destination....I won't be alone.
It will be filled with listeners
Who have time for me and me alone.
Thank God! Never again......all alone!

Shell

It's hard to remember a time there were no tears, no sorrow
  On the surface or hidden just beneath.
It's hard to remember the happy times we had, the sweet love,
  The passion, the poignant memories.
It's easier to remember the bitterness, the hate,
  The disappointments, betrayals, agonies, defeat.

After a time, as with most of us, a shell began to form
  Around my heart and my emotions.
I am afraid of love and happiness for fear
  Of rediscovering the tears.
Until, at night, sometimes I yearn for the refreshing release
  Of being able to shed those tears that lie in wait
Just below the hardened surface of my emotional shell.

Ribbons

I'm bound to earth with ribbons, not chains.
All an enterprising angel needs to do
Is to slip up behind me and untie the bow
And watch the ribbons fly up to the sky
And let this earth-bound body simply—go!

The ribbons are so pretty and so colorful,
They've bound me for so many, many years;
They're silky-soft and flutter in the breeze;
I've loved their anchoring to this life.
They yet permit me to go where'er I please.
But now I'm prepared for that Great Untying.
I'm ready at long last to loose the ribbons
And allow my once-bound body to be free
To soar on wings of angels to my ultimate reward.
Where I will finally utterly, completely just be Me!

Cosmic Plan

Is there some vast cosmic plan
To which we are not privy?
Or did God really set it up
And there's nothing we can do?

Why did we ever marry and
Why that particular one?
Why did we have that child,
Why has it all begun?

Which turn in the road less traveled
Was it I was determined to take?
Which of my many decisions
Is the one I must ultimately make?

Dying, living, working, playing,
Is it really all pre-planned?
Is it all some vague cosmic plan?
Someday we'll understand.

The Thoughts of the Old

I often wonder, as young people do,
Just what 'twould be like to be old;
To have left most of your life behind you,
Like closing tbe book on a tale well told.

I often ponder on the thoughts of the old
As I watch them or hear them talk;
Do they think of the sunshine or of the cold?
I wonder as I walk.

The withered cheek, so wan and cold,
The wrinkled brow with lines of care—
Were they once sweet maids or lads so bold,
These that are now so sad, so spare?

And so I decided to go and ask Grammy;
Surely, I thought, since she's my mother's mother
She must know almost all there could be,
And, being old to me then, I need ask no other.

Then Grammy smiled a smile knowing and wise,
And bade me sit close to her there on the floor.
I watched, and I listened, with widening eyes,
As she opened to me the Past's golden door.

"My child," she began, and her eyes held me fast.
"The thoughts of the old are like those of the young.
They dream of the future, and until the last
Are loath to admit they near life's ladder's last rung.

The dreams of the future are linked with the past,
And, for the old, there may not be a tomorrow
On earth; for today may be the last.
But the thought is not one of sadness or sorrow.

Our memories are those of a younger day,
When life was beginning and dreams were bright.
Happiness abounded—we were young and gay,
And the thought of it ending was a terrible fright!

But not all was joy and not all was gladness;
We sometimes worried—what to eat, what to wear—
For there was care even then, and sometimes sadness,
But the gray clouds soon passed and the weather was fair.

There still remains for us childhood's bright dreams,
Tempered with age and with wisdom now;
Some were merely ridiculous schemes,
But others may someday come true, somehow.

And now, my child, I have grown weary,
For I have poured out my heart and my head to you;
Discard that which has been useless or dreary,
But remember that which was good that I told you."

She leaned back in her chair, and her eyes were gleaming,
The words she had spoken were good and were kind
I wondered if she was still thinking and dreaming,
Her words caught and held there in my mind.

"You asked, my child, what it's like to be old.
Well, perhaps now you know something of it.
Youth is like rubies, but age is like gold:
Youth you enjoy, but age, you will love it.

Do not think too harshly of age, my dear,
Do not wish that you'd never grow old;
Do not relive each day and for each shed a tear,
But live your life as a story well told,

And if, perhaps, you've not finished your task,
Don't be bitter, for it's as it should be.
Go willingly and never a question ask—
Perhaps you're to finish it There, possibly."

I will never forget the things that she told
That day as I sat at her feet on the floor.
I'll understand a bit better the thoughts of the old,
And will not be frightened at the Close of the Door.

I still wonder, as young people do,
Just what 'twould be like to be old,
But I know my thoughts will stay young and true
As I watch my life unfold.

Just When

Just when I think I have finally finished
I start all over again.
Just when I think I have just begun
I come to an end….and then
Whenever I have completed a task
I suspect is really unfinished, and when
It's accomplished to my satisfaction
I seem to begin all over again.

Just when I feel I have slept enough
I begin to yawn and can't stay awake;
When I get into the right pattern again
I'm ever so wakeful—I can't catch a break!
At times there is way too much sleeping,
At times an afternoon nap I must take.
Waking and sleeping—there is no set pattern.
I should get it together, for Heaven's sake!
Troubles come and troubles go and
Just when I am at the end of my rope
A situation occurs leading me to believe
That I am truly without any hope.
Then I feel my way through it
And blindly grope
And manage to overcome it all
And find I can cope.

Just when I am "up" and happy at last,
Confident I know what life is about,
My world's pink and rosy, serene or gay
And I feel that I just want to shout;
It all tumbles down and crashes around me,
And before I know it I begin to pout—
The blue gloom surrounds me;
I once again doubt.
Then the happiness returns,
The depression I can rout.

Just when I believe I have eaten enough
My appetite's triggered anew;
But when I'm hungry and need some food
And don't get it—I am blue.
Whether I'm eating too much or too little,
Can't find that happy medium, true,
When I'm too skinny, when I'm too fat
I just don't seem to have a clue.

This isn't the blues or the doldrums,
This isn't a song about strife,
This isn't a treatise on depression,
Or pain that can cut like a knife.
It's not a philosophical discussion
On the vagaries of my little life;
This isn't even peculiar to me.
It's just about that thing we call LIFE!

I Only Cry In the Shower

I only cry in the shower—
  That's where I go to hide.
I never cry or get upset—
  Because I'm cold.

But I can stand up in the shower
  And turn the water on full-force,
    And yell my heartaches to the heavens,
      And cry my heart out,
        And pray, and praise the Lord,
          And sing to Him;
            And no one hears but me
                        And Him!

Introspection

I am introspective in the morning—
The time between darkness and the dawn,
When sleep has left the building
And duty is poised to come in.
I lie in my warm, cozy nest,
Remembering the days long gone,
And the "what ifs" beg to be let in.

Sometimes the memories are poignant,
Recollection is so very sweet;
A million scenarios run through my brain
And conjecture encases my feet,
It's then that I embrace duty
And rejoice in a life that's complete.

There's little place for introspection
When a life is happy and full.
Tho' everyone sometimes contemplates
That "something else" would be so cool;
To keep aspiring to correction
I'd be twenty-two kinds of a fool!

Traffic Jam

Caught up in the mundane of life, I stalled
In the traffic jam of that great walled
City I considered to be that to which I was called,
And realized suddenly that everything had palled.

I tried to reinvent my goals and somehow recreate
All the possibilities so I could then relate
To what I needed to do to emancipate
My life, my soul, my being, and not procrastinate.

In daily tasks I'm mired—I need rejuvenation;
I must step outside myself to reevaluation
Of all that's now and all that's gone before—a recalculation
To determine how to drive on to my appropriate destination.

Twilight

Twilight's such a poignant time of day,
A bittersweet reminder that night is on its way;
The daylight sighs and wraps her cape
About the lovely shoulders of the landscape;
She knows she will return upon the morrow,
But her adieu holds just a hint of sorrow;
For when she does return, that which remains
Of today will merely be the memory of joys and pains
That yesterday once held, and only now,
In this today, survives the dreams, somehow.

Waiting Is Hard

It's exciting yet sometimes painful,
Growing up's not always fun;
Through trials and tribulations,
When all is said and done,
You try, you strive, you agonize,
You cannot wait until the day
When finally you're a "grownup"
And life will now be going your way.
Waiting's hard.

You just can't wait to be married
To that one special someone,
The other half of your heart,
Your soul mate, your one and only one;
And sometimes it takes a try or two
Before you finally do it right
And meet that perfect person
That makes everything alright.
Waiting's hard.

You're finally going to have a baby!
Wow! Did you ever think you could
Take two less-than-perfect people
And create that miracle that would
Be the best part of the both of you,
That blessed bundle of joy
That seems to make your life complete
Whether it be girl or boy.
But the waiting is hard.

You wait, you pace, you maybe cry—
When will your child come home?
Many sleepless nights are spent
Wondering whither he would roam;
Just out on a date or with a friend,
Maybe painting the town bright red?
Perhaps in service to his country
Not knowing whether alive or dead.
Waiting is very hard.

The trauma of youth is over now,
The middle years even past,
You contemplate your future,
Wondering when you'll go Home at last.
The good, the bad, the indifferent,
It's all the same in the end,
You're longing for your Destiny
And the bright Eternity you'll spend.
Yes, waiting is so hard!

Why Cry?

What in the world makes me cry at Christmas?
Why do I sob when the Holy Spirit touches me?
Why do I weep at military parades?
Why do wedding and births always move me?

When a lover whispers something endearing,
When the Lord gently touches my heart;
When the healing starts, or conviction smarts,
I have crying down to an art.

I guess I'm a weeping Willy—
A soppy, sappy, silly mess.
I cry when I don't even want to
And can't whenever I do.

Mostly, I'm known as hard-hearted—
Or, at least, strong and serene.
Often, I cry deep inside me,
And weep when I can't be seen.

But Christmas and family and sunsets,
I'm obvious in my appreciation
Of the beauty and timelessness.
I pray I'll never reach satiation!

Shattered

Sometimes life doesn't break you
It shatters you like a pane of glass,
Broken into a zillion little pieces,
All a great, vast morass,
Leaving just a pile of shards
Congealing into a gelatinous mass.

It begins with just a miniscule crack
Zigzagging like lightning across the sky.
It can start with the smallest pain
Or be caused by the tiniest lie
Whispered by one you thought loved you,
Shattered beyond wanting to die.

It's an earthquake of such magnitude
It cracks open your entire foundation—
A volcano erupting, spitting lava and fire,
Spewing down without cessation,
A tornado whirling and swirling away,
But when it ceases there is no elation.

Sometimes life must shatter a soul
To begin to fill in the pieces;
To mend all the broken remains
That have scattered to the far reaches;
Then sometime, somewhere, somehow,
Something or Someone finally frees us.

SALUTE TO THE MONTHS

April

März   Mai

Februar   Juni

Januar ——————✦—— Juli

Dezember   August

November   September

Oktober

Tribute to the Months

I really don't mind January,
(In Florida, not up North).
It's a brand-new year, poised upon the brink
Ready to give us all its worth.

In February, I confess I shed a tear—
Valentine's Day without a Valentine.
But it's such a little month
It breezes by in no time.

Now, March is not my favorite month
Even here it's sometimes windy and cold.
It's sort of a waiting-in-Limbo time—
The year's not young but still not old

Sweet, balmy April, and sweeter-still May!
Now that's what I call perfection!
My time and the weather are so sublime,
Every day, every hour, another selection.

What is so rare as a day in June?
I believe that other poet said it all!
The warmth of the sun melts your heart,
Making memories for you to recall.

Dramatic, bombastic, exploding July!
Fireworks, beaches, explosions galore.
Romance and excitement, this month has it all.
July seems to have everything, and more.

August and then September—
For some a period of poignant endings,
Then onward and upward in life
To a season of brand-new beginnings.

What can I say of October, November?
Those glorious, colorful, beautiful days
And nights that are utterly splendid!
I love them both, and all their ways.

But December, ah, December!
The most beloved month of the year.
The past, the present, the future combined
To bring memories of all we hold dear.

January, the Grande Dame

January is the Grande Dame,
Dressed in snowy ermine, quite sophisticated,
Leading all the other months
Ever so enigmatic and complicated.

Whirling and swirling or calm and serene
She must exert herself to try
To overcome December,
The favorite of the twelve.

February

February is the month of love:
Hearts and flowers, bridal showers;
Its very brevity speaks to that:
Short and sweet, complete, replete,
And then delete—so sad.

August is a Lady

Poised between July, her sultry sister,
And September in her flamboyant hues,
August is a lady, dressed in gold and greens and blues:
Blues of bright, translucent skies,
The gold of radiant fields and sun,
The myriad shades of dappled green,
Make the human heart quite undone.

But August is first and foremost
A lady with a past.
History has eschewed its merits:
She's content to come in last,
And stand in the shadows of her sisters—
That infamous character cast
Of some wild and crazy ladies
Whose exploits suggest they may be fast.

But August is a lady
Sometimes quiet, sometimes shy;
But if you're fond of August
No one will ever wonder why.

September

She's vibrant, pulsating, glorious,
The kind of woman you'll remember;
Splashy, vivid color is her trademark.
Often referred to as "Stupendous September".

She dances blithely over the verdant hills,
Part of the sorority of months
Of which she's a charter member.
Never shy, reticent, or retiring,
Ever unforgettable September!

33 YEARS IN PARADISE

Florida Fall

The sun's still shining bright and hot,
You'd never know that Fall is here;
The leaves turn amber in some sun-burnt spot,
That presages the changing of the year,
From blazing, humid, Summer-heated days
To the warm and drier ambiance of Fall.

Awaiting breathlessly the cooler weather,
We yet enjoy this lovely Florida Fall;
Not anticipating cold with any kind of fervor,
Yet relishing cooler breezes, et al.
Content in basking in the sun-drenched days of Autumn,
We eagerly await sensuous Summer's siren call.

Florida Winter

It's Winter now—I'm sad.
The water's too cold to swim—that depresses me.
Oh, some do, I know—it's Florida.

But my body's too pampered for that to appeal to me.
The air is cooler—cold, to me!
But most of the time the sun shines—that makes me happy.

The sun's warm—I'm glad.
My temperament is proportionate to its warmth:
I bask in its healing rays—I exult.

Its glow and heat are vital to my emotional growth;
It's irrational, the importance I place on the sun.
I feel its absence could cause my physical death.

But Winter here is brief—that's great!
I can sometimes even enjoy the difference it makes:
The gray days are few—that's not hard to take.

There are things one can accomplish inside, out of the sun,
Such as writing poems like this.
Then give me Summer *or* Winter—whatever it takes.

Gulf Coast

The Gulf Coast in Summer is something to behold,
It's not like anything else your imagination can boast;
A series of pleasurable sensations you almost can hold.
The warmth of the sunshine, the breeze along the coast,
Epitome of all the beauty of which I've e'er been told.
This little corner of the world that I truly love the most:
The sensuous waters the undulating shores enfold,
The pristine sands to which the seabirds play host,
The myriad of colors, so vibrant, so bold;
The Spanish moss drips from the trees, eerie as a ghost;
The sunsets o'er the ocean, purple, orange and gold.
What a spectacular slice of Paradise this Florida Coast!

My imagination isn't refined enough to tell it all,
Nor my eyesight good enough to see every nuance of it;
My vocabulary's faulty, the proper words I can't recall,
I can only try my best to describe it, bit by bit:
The soaring oaks, the majestic palm trees, oh, so tall,
The poignant panorama when the sights are all moonlit;
One feels so mighty powerful—and yet so very small,
Gazing upward, heaven-ward, as on the beach I sit:
The sea, the sands, the sky—I cannot make the call—
To extol the virtues of this place or say which is my favorite.

West Coast of Florida

The West Coast of Florida is the loveliest place
That I know I have ever beheld;
My thanks to God for living here
Is exuberantly heartfelt!

Palm trees silhouetted against the bright sky,
Their delicate fronds unfurled;
Golden sunshine reflected in water so clear
That you feel you can see the world.

Spectacular panorama of foliage and sea,
The sun tips each wave with gold;
Even on the relatively few gray days,
It's a wonder to behold!

Sea gulls laughing high up above,
Sandpipers toddling along the shore,
My little slice of heaven here on earth—
I just can't ever ask for more!

ON THE MOVE—AGAIN!

It Took a Miracle

It took a miracle to buy a place of my own;
I never dreamed nor even thought of such a thing.
You set more wheels in motion than a big old eighteen-wheeler,
And made me so happy—that's why I sing!

You smoothed out all those pesky wrinkles,
To make that plan of Yours come about;
You did what some said was not possible,
That I could own a home—that's why I shout!

It seems I'm looking a gift horse in the mouth
To say that now I want to sell it and go away;
But now I believe it's time to move again,
And I pray that Satan is not leading me astray!

If it's just my plan I really do not want it,
But if Yours I know You'll make it happen.
I want to be prayed up and ready to do my part,
So the new miracle will not find me nappin'.

And it will surely take another miracle
To make this final relocation come about;
As long as You are not against me
It all will fall in place, I have no doubt.

My Condo

My condo is not pretentious,
It's been built for quite some time—like me.
Not a lot of baths and bedrooms,
Nor fancy frills, you see.

It has withstood hurricanes
And myriad adversities.
It's strong and sturdy, made to last,
Only a few cracks in the foundation—like me.
Perhaps, you'd say, a slight structural challenge?

It has such a peaceful feel about it,
The peace that passes understanding, I say;
The bright colors that I dearly love
Help to hold the doldrums at bay.

College-style bookcases abound—
Fodder for my voracious appetite!
Plants and books and Smiley-Faces
All blend to make my home airy and light.

I love to travel, and visit, and see friends,
But it's always good to return to my little place;
The Lord gave it to me just when needed
And it's filled with His peace and his grace!

My Little Red Apartment

I love my little apartment so high in the sky
So bright and cheerful, colorful and gay;
I can gaze upon the lights of the city at night
And the beautiful vista by day.

I can see the Skyway Bridge and part of the ocean
Or maybe it's just the waterway;
I never tire of the changing scenery—
It's stupendous, that's all I can say.

Inside it's mostly, brightly red—
That's the best I can do with description.
It was certainly just what the doctor ordered—
A definitely surprising prescription!

I wouldn't have dreamed, in my wildest dreams
That someday it would become an addiction,
Loving this little dwelling on the 14th floor
Would not have heretofore been my prediction!

Its hominess, its peacefulness
Gives off a warm and welcome feel;
Folks want to come to visit
And keep me on an even keel.

The affordability of it all,
Of course, just adds to its appeal.
Too many "perks" to enumerate!
All in all, it's quite a deal!

There's others more splendid, as domiciles go,
And some I could get at a better price,
But few I have found in my searches
That I have deemed to be quite as nice.

Of course, there are a few drawbacks,
But that, I think, merely adds to the "spice";
For me, at this time in my life,
My little red apartment will more that suffice.

But Then I Moved—Again!

My little studio is magnificently efficient
I can fool myself into thinking that I am proficient
And that moving has not rendered me somewhat deficient.

It's still a "red" apartment, but with added color,
And so much less expensive—I've saved a pretty dollar,
So making yet another move—I don't see how I can holler.

It's so sweet and cozy and many less steps to take;
So much less housekeeping (tho' the bed's harder to make)
And a clean, efficient oven in which I love to bake,

I asked the Lord to bless it, as I always do,
And I feel the peacefulness here—I have a clue
That the blessing is the reason, don't you?

At any rate I'm happy with the latest move I've made:
As we said when we were young, "I have it made in the shade"!
And even for another this apartment I'd not trade.

There are those who still complain about living here
And who knows where I might be in another year,
But for now I am just as happy as I appear
In my second little red apartment.

Happy Tower

I have a home, way up high,
I call it Happy Tower.
It's not so much the place I live
As the overwhelming sense of power
That I've achieved just living here
And meeting friends and neighbors;
It surpasses all my expectations
And makes it worth my labors.
Perhaps it's more an inner feeling—
Much more than an attitude—
That makes me so profoundly full
Of overwhelming gratitude.
I call it Happy Tower,
My high rise in the sky,
I am so much closer to heaven
I feel that I could fly!
It's just a place to live, you say,
Just a building made of concrete.
But I'm happier here than I've ever been,
And for now, at least, life is sweet-

Moving, Moving

Moving, moving, moving.
What's this thing I have about moving?
Why this compulsion to change my abode?
Why the need to once again hit the road?

It boils down to change, I guess.
To attempting to make a difference
By starting somewhere, somehow, anew,
To try to better my previous performance.

Somehow it seems to stimulate me
When attaining a brand new address;
Something is waiting just around the corner—
Each time I try to make it the best.

A change, a new goal, a new project, if you will,
Perhaps even something of a new identity.
Each time I hope to be a slightly different person
As if a new home can make a new me.

Alas, I find I am always stuck
With the old me and all the old baggage—
"Can't make a silk purse of a sow's ear"—
You know the old adage.

But I still have this thing about moving:
It simply makes me happy!

Never Say Never

I began my life in the mountains.
I may end my life in them, too.
Never say "never" to anything,
Never say vehemently what you won't do.

They say that one man's trash
Is another man's treasure,
And what at one time you hated
May another day bring pleasure.

However, the way my life is going
It seems increasingly clear to me
That I'll be spending the rest of my days
Till the end of my life, near the sea.

And for better, for worse,
For richer or poorer, you see,
This is the place I dearly love
And just where I want to be.

I never saw it coming
The move away from the sea.
But it just goes to show
Never say never, Definitely!

ON WRITING

Collecting Words

I have so many stories in me,
Scenes, ideas and plots,
Outlines in my computer,
Random phrases and sub-plots.

Snippets of dialogue,
Lovely descriptions of scenery,
Sometimes only a word or two,
Hoping my memory will jog.

So why aren't any of them together
In some semblance of order,
Or some effort made to write them down
Or put them in my tape recorder?

Is it fear I cannot finish,
Laziness, apathy, ennui?
Or terror that I'll jot them down
To discover they're not what I want them to be?

All those lovely little words
Dance inside my head,
But putting them all together
Is something I've come to dread.

I've failed before I've started
Because I can't begin
To put them into cohesiveness,
Therefore I'll never win.

Is it simply writer's block
Or a paralyzing fear of rejection
That keeps me jotting all this down,
Or a striving for perfection?

One day I may conquer fear
And finally write that story;
I long to marshal all those words
Into something besides poetry.

Until then I will keep on
Jotting thoughts, making notes,
Ever imagining deathless prose
And collecting immortal quotes.

No Writer Am I

I once proclaimed to the world, "I am a writer!
I was so proud and adamant about it all,
Perhaps I was endeavoring to convince myself,
But I knew one day my fairy-tale castle would fall!

I was proud of the things I had written—still am!
And collected unfinished manuscripts galore;
I was happy with what I had accomplished,
But sad no publishers were beating down my door.

Now, in the winter of my long life
I have finally come to grips with reality.
I really don't deserve to call myself a writer,
Perhaps I never really had it in me.

I still call myself a poet, in humbleness and pride.
I will never give up on the gift God gave me.
So I will continue to write my little verses
And always and ever call it poetry.

On and On and On

This is the time I should be writing,
I have so much I want to say;
And seemingly not much I can do
To fill my time and fill my day.

Another poem? I hear you say.
If I add it to my latest book
It will soon consist of a thousand pages!
I couldn't bind that by hook or by crook.

So, I guess I'll just write when I feel led,
Letting my little fat fingers ramble
Over the keyboard so fleet and quick,
Writing is always something of a gamble.

It's assuming that anyone wants to read
Anything else I want to write;
But what other pastime do I have?
I'll continue as long as I have my sight.

It's simply a catharsis, this writing bit,
It's just another way of journaling;
I keep on putting my thoughts down on paper,
And it seems that lately it's spiraling.

So, please bear with me, one and all,
Whoever happens upon these lines.
Just know that the thoughts are all my own,
Whether or not they can be deemed rhymes.

Maybe I'll go on from here,
At least I will make this open-end,
In order to save room for more thoughts,
And I feel very sure they will not end.

On Writing Verse

Whether it makes sense or not at the time,
Sometimes I just hanker to write verse;
To put on paper line after line—
I could, most likely, do better, but also do worse.

There are just some occasions that lend themselves
To writing simple poems, rhyme after rhyme;
Lines that are witty, or sometimes profound,
Or times, all too few, something sublime.

Oh, to write verses of passion, or lines to soothe,
Longing that something of consequence I might achieve!
That's my most magnificent obsession,
And the culmination of my desires, I believe!

But whether I ever write that poem extraordinaire;
That one in a million I may one day compose,
I must still keep on writing my verse,
Not for the reader to judge, I suppose.

Write On

My hand aches, my fingers are numb,
But still I have to write
On and on ad infinitum!
You can recognize my plight.

Sometimes early, sometimes late,
Sometimes far into the night,
Until my penmanship is illegible—
Then the computer makes it right.

Sometimes gay, sometimes morose,
It can be witty, occasionally bright,
Funny or sad or quite profound,
It all turns our alright.

At times I'm not happy with all the words
Sometimes they're a sheer delight;
Once in a while I can't seem to stop,
There seems to be no end in sight.

I'm trying to cease this "ite" kick,
I'm trying with all my might!
I will desperately seek to stop this—
I'm putting up quite a good fight!

Forced Writing

I haven't written a poem for a while,
Not one of particular importance,
Or one to evoke some bile.
Even one to bring forth a chuckle,
A guffaw or a little smile.
Oh, yes there's the one for a gift,
One to send as a gift tag
I wrote to accompany a present,
But that sort of counts as a gag.
Not that the gift is at all funny
But that the verse is mere doggerel,
Written with love and kisses,
But not written at all well.
But why don't I feel led to write of late?
Am I just too busy to do so?
Heaven knows I'm not penning a great novel
Or exploring like Robinson Crusoe!
There's nothing momentous occurring,
My life is really quite mundane;
But that very fact should produce more—
All this free time should bring gain.
Perhaps I only write when I'm pressured,
Maybe my un-busy state creates ennui.
So you're saying I just shouldn't force it
Or something like this comes to be!

Why Write?

Writing, writing, ever writing, fingers flowing o'er the keys.
Sometimes thinking, hardly thinking, sometimes agonizing
                o'er the words.
Never stopping, seldom stopping, often flowing with great ease.
At times quitting, stopping for hours or whole days at a time.
What does God have in store for me and my expertise?
What, really, **is** my area of expertise?

I research, I edit, I type another man's words well.
What do I actually ever say for myself?
But writing I must—the Muse doth compel;
Does it really matter what I write, what I say?
Do I, in turn, have a story to tell?
Or do I merely write to be writing, to be doing?

I continue to jot down my simple poetry.
It just flows from my fingertips and on to my computer.
The words are my life, the essence of Me.
If no one ever reads what I write, so be it.
You have told me, Lord, to just write for You.
So, I did, and I do, and I will!

I Write Because

All my life I thought I'd be a writer—
Novel, short story, romance, essay.
All my life I desired to become a writer,
But never sat down to journal every day.

Since early childhood I called myself a writer
A most prolific author—without pay!

Then my efforts turned from prose to poetry,
With a few exceptions I won't note.

My poems range from age of 10 to present;
I diligently enter all those that I wrote
Into my friend, my confidante, my computer,
Even those I readily can quote.

But still there is a yearning deep inside me
To fulfill that dream to one day write a book.
Whether for my own self aggrandizement
Or for my progeny to one day look
Back at the accomplishment of Mother,
And be proud of what their Mama undertook.

I don't know …. but now I write
Just what the muse has prompted me to write.
If editing other peoples' books, so be it
That novel may have been too big a bite!
Or turning humdrum happening into verse—
I write because I write and that's alright!

Modern Poets

I read a quote that implied that
  Modern poets were insipid and
    Had nothing to say—I disagree!

If that's because those "old boys" and girls
  Used a vocabulary we nowadays
    Are hard-pressed to understand—I agree.

Modern English has definitely deteriorated—
  Perhaps terminally. But I don't agree
    That we no longer have anything profound to say
      Or communicate how we feel—I disagree!

We love, we laugh, we philosophize and think
  As well as any of the poets of former centuries
    But now you have no doubt of what we're saying!

But there must be some addendum here
  Regarding those whose "modern" vocabulary
    Includes the ribald, the coarse, the raw—
      I don't consider them poets!

I agree they have nothing of importance to say
  And no adequate vocabulary with which to convey it,
    So maybe the original indictment against modern poetry
      Was partially right, after all.

A Million Stories

There's a million stories locked inside my brain so tight:
Those I've read and those I've seen and those I want to write.
Many times I write all day and far into the night,
Most of which will never appear, tho' I try with all my might
To give them birth and finally let them see the light.
I've come to grips with all of this and realize it's alright.
Yet I do still battle and strain and push and wrestle and fight
For I feel that someday, sometime, something will incite
That spark of inspiration that will make me higher than a kite,
And once again remove all the evidence of my plight
By permitting me to finish what I started—but not quite.

INSPIRATIONAL

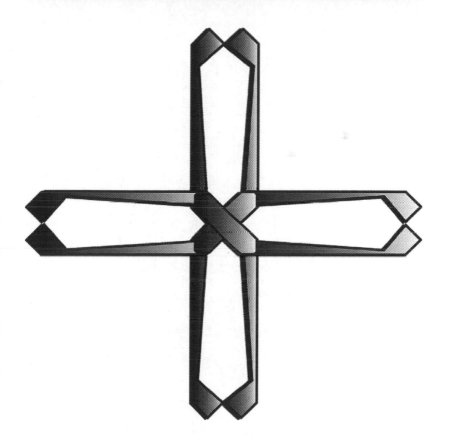

Flying High

Flying high above the clouds,
Sundown fast approaching;
Cotton candy clouds my carpet,
Sapphire night encroaching,

Horizon stretching far afield,
Golden streaks across the sky;
From my vantage point I trace
This gigantic silver bird I fly,

The silver stars are twinkling above,
The lights of cities sparkle below;
Now it's completely dark, totally night,
We're basking now in moon glow.

Flying high with the world at my feet,
The universe arrayed from this small window,
The experience once felt I want to repeat,
And remember when I finally land below.

Don't Call Me by Name

Don't call Me Lord
  If you don't even know Me!
Don't say to Me, "Jesus…."
  As one would to a friend;
If you don't even know Me,
  Or we're barely acquainted,
Don't call Me by Name.

Don't call Me Master
  If you're not My slave,
If you don't bow before Me
  Or tremble at My power,
If you don't even obey Me
  Don't call Me by Name.

Don't call Me Savior—
  That means that I've saved you.
Don't say that I have
  If you don't really believe.
If you haven't even asked Me,
  Or haven't repented,
Don't call Me Redeemer.

Don't call Me Jesus
  If you don't really love Me!
Don't you know how indifference
  Makes My heart break?
Just love Me, My children,
  And love God, Our Father,
And Call Me by Name.

Answer Me

How come You always answer me
Before I even ask?
How come You're there to help me
With each and every task?

I seldom ever talk to You
Or even call Your name;
But before I think to ask You
You answer all the same.

How come You think I'm worth
All the things You do for me?
The trouble that I put You through!
You surely must agree.

I'm not asking 'cause I'm humble—
That's one thing I'll never be.
I just really want to know, Lord,
Why You always answer me?

Dear Martha

When I finally get to heaven there's one thing I intend to do:
I plan to curl up on a big white cloud and talk to a certain few.
I'll plump up that fluffy pillow, make it nice and comfortable,
And have a heart to heart with Martha, as long as she is able.

I want to tell you, Martha, how much I empathize
And even identify with you much of the time.
I've very often wondered if you forgave Mary?
Making you do all the work surely was a crime.

It's so hard to be "the strong one", the "doer" all the time!
It would at times be oh, so nice, to sit at Jesus' feet
And feel that was your rightful place in the world.
That would have made my life replete.

God made us each a certain way, and we must conform;
While Mary had the better place, we are important, too.
We no doubt should have learned to compromise,
To learn to listen as well as to "do".

Martha, I know you've achieved that balance now,
Though it took a little while to gain it;
I pray that one day I will, too,
And not always have to strain it.

Martha, I'd really like to talk to you
And see what you have gleaned
From living with Mary and Lazarus
And on Jesus to have leaned.

I think that in you I have found a friend,
A veritable bedfellow;
I suppose that wisdom comes with age,
Or comfort makes me mellow.

I do admire your diligence, Martha, but
I'll try to be a bit like Mary, too;
I want so to be like she was, but
I know my penchant is to be like you

I Can't Be Still

"Be still and know I am Lord."
Easy for You to say, Lord,
But I cannot stay still for very long!
I am always going, doing,
Saying, thinking, wishing, wanting.
Is that so very wrong?
I feel the compulsion to be moving,
Planning, organizing, prioritizing,
Needing to do more and more and more.
I say I have two modes:
Doing and sleeping!
But movement seems to be at my core;
Even in sleep I dream,
I plot and plan and strategize.
And now, it seems, I'm sleeping more.
Be still? I don't think I know how
To not do anything!
I believe You mean to know You
In the midst of everything.
No matter what I'm doing or saying,
Whether asleep or awake
I know You.

What a Beautiful God-Given Day

What a beautiful, God-given day it is,
What a wonderful, heaven-sent day;
God's in His heaven and smiling at me,
Lovingly, tenderly smiling at me.

What a bright, happy, sunshiny day it can be,
When Jesus is right by your side;
Your steps will not lag when you go on your way,
Laughing and happy, with nothing to hide.

What a beautiful, God-given evening it is,
And the cares of the day are behind;
You've asked and you've received,
Trusted and believed,
This beautiful, God-given day.

Could It Be Now?

Could it be now
That we hear the first blast of the trumpet
That we see the lightening of the eastern sky?
Could it be now
We see the first glimpse of Jesus
Stepping out upon the clouds on high?

Are we ready to receive such a sight—
The blazing sun splitting the night?
Are we really ready to meet Jesus?
Will we rejoice when first He sees us?
Or fall prostrate on our very faces,
Feeling unworthy to accept His graces
Appalled that we have not done what we should,
Not even all the things we genuinely would?

Could it be now?
Can we conceive of it?
Are we looking upward with joy
To anticipate this ultimate climax
To all that we have thought and prayed
And dreamed of since we knew Him?
Could it be now?
Even so, Lord Jesus, come!

Your Eyes Will See the King

Your eyes will see the King in all His beauty.
They will behold a far and distant land.
Open your eyes to all the beauty
He holds within the palm of His hand.

For you shall see the New Jerusalem,
Which He has made to be His habitation,
Where we will dwell with Him in truth and beauty:
In Exultation, and Jubilation,
That far and distant land is close at hand!

I Give it All to You

Lord, I offer it all to You,
The questions, the answers,
The prayers I pray for someone else,
I give it all to You.

The problems, the troubles,
The things I want for myself,
I give them all to You—
What else can I do?

They're all Yours, anyway,
What more can I say?
But to give them all to You today.
Don't let me grab them back again tomorrow.

It's all in Your hands,
Help me to understand
That I've given it all to You.

Let me bask in Your presence
Rest in Your peace,
Knowing I can trust in You,
Lord, I give it all to You.

In Charge

I am walking by the streams of living water,
Wandering on the beaches of my soul,
Strolling on the seashore with my Savior,
For I know that it is He who makes me whole.

Walking hand in hand with Jesus,
Knowing He will never let me go;
Wind and wave may buffet my body,
But I'm confident that He's in control.

The storms of life may sometimes overwhelm me,
Everything may not always seem serene;
But through my tears I'll feel His gentle guidance.
How can such a mighty Presence be unseen?

And when the storm is over and the sun shines,
I will once again be skipping by the sea;
Hand in hand with Him I'll see Him smile—
We're both so glad I let Him be in charge of me.

I Have Chosen You

I have chosen you to be My own.
Before the world began, you I have known.
  I will mold you, and make you
  A vessel useful to Me.
For I have chosen you to be My own.

Why have You chosen me to be Your own?
I am unworthy, Lord, that You have known.
  I've denied You, defied You,
  And done what I wanted to do.
Why have You chosen me to be Your own?

Thank God You've chosen me to be Your own!
I am so grateful, Lord, You must have known.
  Please mold me and make me
  A vessel useful to You.
Thank God You've chosen me to be Your own!

Be Still

I have known love and I have known passion,
I have known what it is to have loved;
I have risen above trials, tribulations and heartaches,
I have gone through myriad battles.
And God has shown me I have what it takes.
With His help I have come out into the sunlight
Of His marvelous blessings.

I have known that special "high on life" feeling,
That euphoric sensation when you know
You are close to Him—in His presence,
In His arms and in His will.
I yearn to remain just resting in Him,
And so, I will pause, and be still.

He Is Risen

He is risen! He is risen, indeed!
Not just Easter Sunday, but today;
He is here for each of us, if we but heed;
He is ever here in every way.

He was not risen, in the past tense,
Not just *was* risen but *is* risen, indeed!
In every manner that we can and cannot sense.
Jesus is risen, He is risen indeed!

Have you experienced that truth?
Do you know that you know that you know?
If you love Him, will you be as Ruth
And say, "Whither Thou goest I will go"?

Even if you don't, He s risen, indeed!

When I Take My Eyes off You

When I take my eyes off You I fall.
When I look at You I walk on water.
When I take my eyes off You I fall
And nearly drown.

When I take my eyes off You I fall.
If I'd only look at You each minute of the day
   I could walk on water,
   I could move a mountain,
I could be the person You want me to be.
When I look at You I can do anything.

Hey, Dad

No earthly one to talk to,
So I'll talk to You, instead
I'm a little "under the weather"—
Had to get out of bed.

I needn't tell You all my thoughts,
That really does go without saying,
But I need to bare my heart to You—
Some folks just call it praying.

I want to remind You that I love You,
And whatever You do is fine.
Heal me, test me, take me Home,
I'm content with Your will divine.

You gave me the gift of poetry
So choosing this way is appealing;
Call it talking, praying, communication,
At least I know with Whom I'm dealing.

I'm grateful for all You've done for me
And what You'll do in the future;
I've never been one for glamour and glitz,
Not for me the haute couture.

Just keep me nestled under Your heart,
Closely cuddled up by Your side.
Grant me Your comfort, peace and joy,
In Your shadow I will happily abide.

I Want to Be Led

I want to be led by the Holy Spirit,
I want to be shown what and how to do it;
I want to know without the shadow of a doubt
That it's what Jesus wants me to do,

I want a clear leading from the Lord,
I want the strength to follow through,
I want to know for certain what I'm doing really pleases God,
I want to know it pleases Jesus, too.

I want to be led by the Holy Spirit,
I want to be shown what and how to do it;
I want to know without the shadow of a doubt
That it's what Jesus would have me do.

God Laughs

Don't you sometimes hear God chuckling in the breeze?
Or gurgling in the rushing mountain stream?
Or laughing right out loud in a cheerful sort of way,
When a summer storm blows up from out of nowhere?

Can't you just see Him smiling fondly at the antics of His children;
Or the sweet, sad smile when we are naughty?
Oh, I know some think of God as a serious, sober statesman,
Ruling o'er the earth with reign of iron,

Coming down on all of us;
With a frightening fury when we dare step a
Fraction out of line—not me!
I know I often hear God laugh.

I know my God is awesome, but His rule is not by fear.
He's a loving, gentle parent, wanting only what is best
For me and everyone concerned.
And I can trust Him to take care of me.

As with my earthly father, my uppermost desire
Is to do whatever makes Him smile.
I cherish every moment that in precious camaraderie
Not only can I hear God laugh, I know He laughs with me.

How I love to hear God laugh!

Doubter

Hey there, Doubter, what are you doing?
You know who I AM but your doubts keep accruing.
You've loved Me for a long time,
You've accepted Me for the upward climb
Yet still you are a Doubter, and that's not the thing to do.
Hey there, little Doubter, what makes you think it's cool
To have a niggling little doubt? That's more than being a fool!
You can't believe Me one day and then doubt Me the next;
You are exceedingly inconsistent, and with you I'm very vexed!
So tell Me, little Doubter, what you intend to do.

I Wish Jesus Had Arms

I often wish that Jesus had arms
And that He'd put them gently around me;
Oh, I sometimes feel His presence overwhelm
Me and know, as always it surrounds me,
But I wish that I could really feel His arms
And feel His breath so sweet upon my cheek.
I long to feel His tangible flesh upon me
And experience His awesome love, unique.
I know I should be happy, knowing He is here
But sometimes when life just seems way too tough
I really wish to feel His loving arms around me
And truly feel that His love is enough.
I'll always wish that Jesus had real arms!

Today Is Yours

Today is yours!

To cry out loud or
To be too proud
To let anyone know how you feel.

To laugh at a prank,
Or be willing to thank
God for bringing you through your ordeal.

You can champ at the bit
And swear you won't fit
Into the mold that you desire.

Or let God do
What He wants to you,
And mold you in the refiner's fire.

You can scream and shout
Or laugh and sing about
The circumstance coming your way.

It's your decision,
You can make the revision
By the minute or hour or day.

When I Get Myself Out of the Way

Jesus, I'm growing fonder of You.
Jesus, I like You better each day.
Jesus, I could even learn to love You,
If I could get myself out of the way.

Savior, I now appreciate You.
Master, I've even learned to obey.
My Lord, I love You more every day
The more I get myself out of the way.

Lap of God

I long to curl up in the lap of God,
To snuggle contentedly 'neath His heart;
To have Him tenderly wipe away my tears,
And lovingly, patiently, His wisdom impart.

I yearn to feel His loving arms around me.
I can almost feel His hand upon my shoulder.
I know that when I am away from Him
My body, my life, my soul grows colder.

Oh, may I ever spend my time with Him,
All my days, till I'm beneath the sod;
Then nestle throughout eternity,
Resting peacefully upon the lap of God.

Where Will I Be?

Where will I be in ten more years?
Polishing the hinges on the pearly gate?
Sitting at the feet of Jesus
Listening to Him explain what we once thought of as fate?

Where will I be in five more years?
Wishing I was in the scenario above
Or trying still to do my best
To make a difference to those I love?

Where will I be in two more years?
Only He knows what I'll be doing and saying
I can dream and conjecture all I want,
I just want to be obeying.

Where will I be in another day
Or week or month or year?
I just want to know I belong to Him
And that He can wipe away any tear.

I may be happy and mightily healed
And working diligently for Him;
But wherever I am, in whatever state,
I WILL be obeying and loving Him!
Thank You, Jesus!

Glorious Sunrise

My heart exults in Your glorious sunrise,
My senses reel in Your wondrous day;
My emotions soar beholding Your skies,
I must sing of the beauty of Your ways.

I wonder why early man didn't know it was You
That created this marvelous orb called the sun?
The glory, the majesty, the beauty of it should
Be evidence that You were the One!

Talk To Me

Talk to me, oh, talk to me
In the wee small hours of the night.
Talk to me, talk to me
In the deep recesses of my soul.
Talk to me, talk to me,
Tell me of the secrets of the universe.
Talk to me, talk to me,
And tell me of my role.

Talk to me, Lord,
Let me hear Your voice
Thundering in my heart!
Let me know your ways,
Let me make my choice,
Tell me of my part.
Talk to me, talk to me,
Whisper of the love we share.
Talk to me, now and evermore.

Resurrection Day

Easter isn't bunnies
Or colored Easter eggs—
It's Jesus.

Easter isn't pageants
Or marvelous cantatas—
It's Jesus.

He came to earth
For such a time as this;
He came, He died, He rose again
So all of us might live
In the glorious certainty
Of Resurrection Day.

He lived for us
He died for us
He was resurrected to prove
That He truly is the Messiah.

Accept His sacrifice again.
Rededicate yourself to Him
On Resurrection Day.......and Always!

Ready

There's a current Christian song
That really sums it up:
"I'm not unhappy but I'd take the train today
If You'd come get me,"
Perhaps just plain tired is what I feel.
I've lived so long that nothing now seems real.
No, I'm not unhappy or distressed;
Mostly I am joyful and unstressed.

But there's not the same feeling of goals
That used to govern my life as it rolls
Along, ever hastening to that ultimate end—
Heaven is lying just beyond the bend.
Tasks all seemingly will never be completed,
My time and energy have simply been depleted.
The sunniest of worlds brightens my days,
But I've gone from vivid hues to shades of gray.

I've never felt I'd see the Rapture of the Church.
I always thought I'd go and leave the rest in the lurch;
But now I'm not so sure, it seems it may be time
For Jesus to come back for me, and I'm
So ready to go with Him—bus or plane or train—
Or caught up in a twinkling. Heaven I will gain
And yet, I wish that I'd done so much more
To give to Him and even up the score.

I know, rationally, that I really never could
Do more than He has in mind for me that I would
Be able and willing to do for Him in the time
Allotted to me. I sometimes feel like a mime—
Just making the motions of a Christian life,
Keeping my head just above the water of its strife,
But not really doing or being what He wants of me.
I want so to do more before entering Eternity,
But if this is His way of preparing me for Glory,
Who am I to argue with this age-old story?

Yes, I am not unhappy, but I'd take His hand today
To join Him in the clouds of gold and blue and gray,
To live with Him for always and forever,
Up there where all the Saints will gather!

The "Quit" Button

I suddenly found within myself a "Quit" button—
Somehow, somewhere and to my great surprise!
I never ever knew that it was there before—
It certainly was a master of disguise.

I suppose everyone has a "Quit" button, too,
And perhaps some, on it, rely;
I just felt that I no longer wanted to go on,
All the gumption that I thought I had was a lie.

I desired nothing greater than to push that button—
It wasn't even a negative emotion that I felt;
Just a profound inevitability that I would quit
The thoughts, demands and problems with which I dealt.

I could so quickly, quietly, easily push that button
Just to see all the turmoil and turbulence be quelled.
But would God want me to use that option,
Or would He be profoundly repelled?

I know where I am going and with Whom,
So I know that peace and joy's my destination.
I also know that this is not the answer:
To push the button without a moment's hesitation.

I know that God didn't put that "Quit" button in me!
It's something that just is—like gravitation.
The most amazing thing was its discovery;
I never even knew I had it in me.

I'm strong, I'm tried, I'm true, I am a pillar,
But sometimes life just presses in upon me,
And I am really tempted to push the button
That would release me from my own mortality.

To push or not to push, that is the question
That I'm faced with at least every other day;
But I know that deep within me is His strength
And I know that there is always a better way.
To deal with all the tests and circumstances.
And, so, I will not PUSH, instead, I'll PRAY!

Prisoner of Hate

No more will I roam through the fields of golden grain,
No more will I enjoy the soft sounds of the rain;
I shall never wander along that shadowy lane,
For I shall never, ever, return there again.

Gone for me all blissful thought and wonderful sensation,
From strife and toil I can never expect a very long vacation;
For I am the victim of my own detestation
I am the restrictor of my own emancipation.

Deep down in my subconscious heart a dormant fire lay;
But it all too often springeth forth from day to day;
And I have never yet learned how to pray
To the Dear Father, for hope's last ray.

Someday, perhaps, I shall break the chains that bind me,
And with God's help, my eyes will truly see.
I shall no more searching, seeking, blindly groping be;
Then, perhaps, I'll have the chance to sail that Heavenly sea.

So, until then, patiently I'll wait
Until my soul enters that golden gate.
Then I never again be the marionette of Fate,
And I shall never find myself the Prisoner of Hate.

Pity Party

I'm having a pity party
And even God is invited!
He knows that I won't stay there
Long enough to be indicted
By the overwhelming feeling
That my world is closing in;
I realize tarrying at the party
Would be akin to sin.

So, sometimes a pity party
Is what the Doctor ordered.
Cry awhile—let it all out—
Even ranting and raving may be supported.
Everyone needs a good cry now and then
And He fully understands it,
For you are never really alone—
After all, He invented it!

No Fair

"No fair!" he shouted, shaking his fist at God.
"No fair!" like a little boy wanting his own way.
Life just wasn't treating him
The way he thought it should.

"Life isn't fair!" she cried, when all answers seemed to be "No!"
"Nothing's going the way I know it should.
I say my prayers and do what's right—
I *know* that I've been good."

He might have just refused to pay our ransom—
"No fair!" He could have cried in the Garden of Gethsemane.
He could have told His Father, "They're not worth it!
I can't endure that cross at Calvary."

Now, can you still cry out, "No fair?"

Necessity

"I am Necessity," stated the wraith.
"How are you going to care for me?
What are you doing to prepare the way
To make me your paramount priority?
How do you suppose you will manage
To expedite all my needs this day;
To assure that I'm well taken care of,
For I am Necessity!"

"I am not wont to allow you to forget
That you must grant obeisance to me.
You don't even have time for Invention—
In your life I am the top priority.
I will not let you go or relieve you.
I have your life by the throat, so to speak.
You are mine, no escape, no turning away,
For I am Necessity!"

But God is my Provider, Necessity,
And I don't even know your name.

My Heart Is a Prayer

Lord, my heart is all a prayer,
But now it's silent unto You;
I am too tired to search for words,
I rest upon Your sympathy;
To understand when I am dumb;
Well I know You still hear me.

I know you hear me because
A quiet peace inundates me,
And fills the places where before
Weak thoughts were wandering wearily.
Deep within me it is calm,
Though waves are tossing outwardly.

Sometimes I simply cannot grasp
The prayerful phrase I feel I should emote;
I just don't seem to have the power
To pray; except something by rote.

My lips, my mind, my heart is totally
Involved with simply breathing; so there's
Such comfort in the knowledge that You know
My heart is one all-encompassing prayer!

My Psalm

Oh, Lord, I feel like a Psalmist,
Praising Your holy name.
Extolling Your marvelous virtues,
Your mercies ever the same.

I kneel in adoration,
I stand in awe of You,
I raise my hands to Your glory
To give You the honor You're due.

My Lord, You have always known me
From my mother's womb to now.
My gifts, my very life,
You marvelously endow.

If I could play and sing,
I would do it all for You.
So, accept my fumbling words,
You are eminently due.

Your grace, Your mercy and kindness,
Have followed me all my days.
Your awesome majesty I perceive,
May I glorify You in all ways.

My love and esteem are Yours, Lord,
Along with my profound adoration.
I praise You, Almighty God
With joyous exultation!

My Bleeding Soul

My soul is torn and bleeding, Lord,
My mind and spirit cast adrift
Upon a surging, pulsing sea of adversity.
My body's bruised and tortured, too;
There's no respite from the torments
Of care, and chaos and calamity—
    Except in You,

Nowhere is there a friend to mind
The mind the trouble I am undergoing,
Although some try to help me through.
I can't articulate the thoughts and feelings
Coursing through my being.
I whirl and turn, I know not what to do—
    Except to give it all to You.

As Job, I see my life in utter chaos,
Not feeling condemned, but
Knowing that the Evil One is drawing nigh.
He's ever after my soul, and hence my family
Will be tried and tested, maimed and mutilated,
Beyond anything I can imagine or conceive.
If they are being tested, too, so be it.
I know we will survive, and
    Cross our own Red Sea to You.

I cry to You, my God, cease testing!
The lessons you have shown us all are clear;
We WILL be Yours! We WILL be consecrated!
Wholly and Holy unto You!
Bind up the wounds that Satan has inflicted.
No! Heal them wholly and completely, now!
But I will praise You now and ever after.
I will ever praise You and adore You.
As the three Hebrew children, I will declare:
My God can deliver me and mine—
But should He not—
    I'll still adore You and believe.

One day soon we all will gather,
Individually and/or corporately, we'll worship You.
E'en now we all can say, I praise You, Jesus,
For You, alone, know the beginning from the end.
You, alone, will someday make it clear
Why all of this has come to persecute your children
And make this bleeding soul to question, "Why?"
You alone are worthy of our praise amid this tribulation,
You alone can make the bitter into sweetness,
And turn disaster into something dear
    If we but stand firm in You.

Pete Was Quite a Guy!

Pete was a man after my own heart:
He called a spade a spade.
Stalwart, vigorous, down-to-earth
He made a plan and the plan was laid.

He knew what he wanted,
At least most of the time,
And set about going after it
When at times it was quite a climb.

He was above all a mortal man
Who had his faults, as we all do;
His biggest mistake, denying the Lord,
Was one he would always rue.

But when God's Holy Spirit
Took control he was over powered;
And from that time on, with
God's anointing, he was showered.

Good old Pete, he taught us true,
The ways of the Lord stand forever.
Tho' men, as the grass, will wither and fall,
We can stand strong if we endeavor.

A fisherman of some renown,
His reputation spread from town to town,
He even walked upon the sea
When Jesus bade—tho' briefly!

Pete reminded us Jesus is the cornerstone,
And those who trust Him will not be put to shame;
We are a chosen people and if we
Follow Him, will never be the same.

So, Pete, the humble fisherman,
To call him a coward would be a blunder;
He became Simon Peter, Apostle of Christ!
Which made him great—and no wonder!

Lowly to Lovely

How can something so horrible be holy?
How can an emblem of destruction
Be converted to a piece of jewelry?
How can anything so lowly become lovely??

Man, born to be cursed and die
Can become a Godly creation,
Born again to follow the Lord Jesus Christ,
And be a part of a great Christian nation.

The cross designed for death and torture,
Has become the Christian symbol of love;
The logo of the people of God,
Worn to embellish throats and homes.

Thus it proves that many things have meaning
Beyond the obvious, surface evidence;
Analyzing it all is counter-productive.
Suffice it to say, it's because God made it so!

Loneliness

Loneliness is just a way of getting your attention.
Loneliness is just a means of
Bringing you before the Lord.
Being alone isn't always lonely,
To be lonely you needn't be alone.
Recognize the One who loves you
Is craving your attention—
He is only using this to bring you close to Him.
Jesus loved you so much He died for you.
Do you love Him enough to accept that as true?

Overwhelmed

Would I be overwhelmed with joy,
As the young teen-aged girl was, they say?
Or would I be burdened down with grief
That my well-planned life was o'er?
How could I convince a man
Of the virgin that I truly was
When all the evidence was
So overwhelmingly against me?
How could even such a godly man
Believe I told the truth—
That I had been touched by the Holy Spirit?
How could anyone believe that?
Why would my family and friends,
My dear Mother and Father
Choose to believe a young girl's story
Of an angel's visitation and
That God had chosen her to be
The mother of the Blessed Messiah?
That was blatant nonsense, pure and simple!
No one would—or could—believe that!
But they could—and they did—and Mary
Was the Mother of our Savior, Jesus Christ!
But I still wonder if I would have believed
And accepted the angel's proclamation?
Perhaps the answer always lies
In how close one is to God.

Reverse the Curse

That is a phrase I have heard all my life,
And wasn't quite sure what it meant.
But now I can say what it means to me,
With the answer I'm quite content.

I was aging and really expecting to die
When God intervened in my life.
For whatever reason, it wasn't my time,
I suppose I was slated for a bit more strife.

But instead, I seem to be reversing the curse,
So to speak, as I seem to grow younger
With each passing day I regain part of my youth
I seem to be growing better and stronger.

Now, my physical being hasn't changed
So much as my attitude, I suppose.
For what Satan planned for evil for me
Became turned to good, God knows.

One should not really live by feelings alone
But my feelings are really quite changed
I simply "feel" much younger and stronger
And my whole life has been rearranged.

At least now, when God takes me home
I believe I've accomplished a bit more
Than if I'd have gone on a few years ago
And my time here would have ended before.

I know that I've learned a few lessons,
In obedience, trust and just letting go.
There's been a profound change in me
And I hope it's been seen by others I know.

The curse was old-age and infirmity
But now, thanks to Him, I know better.
I swallowed it hook, line and sinker but
He's reversed the curse to the letter!

Relinquishment

My life changed completely, and for the better
When I let go of conjecture and relinquished it all
To the God of the universe, omniscient One,
Who knows when I climb and sees when I fall.

Who is in charge of my comings and goings
And orchestrates even my daily breaths;
Who rules and reigns within my heart
And prods me to do my very best.

When my mind is stayed upon Him, as it were,
My best comes much easier than my worst,
All actions and thoughts are focused on Him
I've made Him my Alpha—always my first.

When I took Him as Lord and Messiah
My very countenance was brightened;
As I read and pondered upon His word,
My very heart was lightened.

When I willingly gave up my life to Him,
When I died to myself I was born again.
Nothing can separate me from Jesus
I relinquished myself to the "Hound of Heaven"!

Mother Eve, You Blew It!

I'm sorry to say, I don't like my gender,
They are not always nice, and certainly not fair.
Women are born to be actresses,
And do what most men wouldn't dare.

They wheedle, and whine, and cry,
And are really brought up to deceive;
It's not merely my own opinion,
It's been true since Mother Eve.

Yes, I have loved several women,
Chiefly my Mother and Aunt.
My Mom was, undoubtedly, a saint.
But to say my Aunt was, I just can't.

My daughters are really wonderful,
My daughters-in-law truly good,
But to state that any are perfect
I just wouldn't if I could.

Every little girl is taught to play games
And wrap little boys 'round their finger;
Even the homeliest of girls, it seems
Can learn how to make a man linger.

I guess that's one subject I never mastered:
I would have made "D"s in flirting.
'Tho I made a few conquests,
It was I that was left with the hurting.

Oh, Mother Eve, you did a disservice
To womankind everywhere.
You taught us deceit with our weaning
And to comb in allure with our hair.

You would never believe what we've come to,
The Mom of the whole human race!
We just never quite "got it"—
That which you did with such style and grace.

I'm afraid, as a sex, we've not done well.
We barter and hint and cajole.
We're so seldom truthful and honest;
We're really a mess, as a whole!

Mostly, we're only hurting ourselves,
But sometimes others may suffer;
It's a shame, but before it's all over,
Everyone loses, we discover.

Oh, to be truly pure and ingenuous!
What I'd give to be honest and open!
How I yearn to be the me God wants me to be
And not merely going on copin'!

It's really no fun, this going through life
Deceiving and grasping and gropin';
We'd all rather be transparent!
Until then, I'll simply say, "Here's hopin'!"

FAMILY

Nameless Thing

My heart is filled with a nameless thing
    That I just can't classify;
My eyes fill with tears, yet it quiets my fears,
    There's a lump in my throat when I try.

Perhaps it is joy, or surprise, or respect
    Or maybe it's just that day or night
She's there beside me no matter what,
    To chase away pain and sickness and fright.

But I suppose that the nameless thing
    So deep in my heart is love.
For there's no one quite like a Mother, and mine
    Makes the earth as sweet as Heaven above.

Farewell, Alma Mater

Farewell, Alma Mater, farewell to thee;
You know and I know, what you have meant to me.
Your strong and hallowed walls have sheltered me,
Your long and teeming halls have harbored me;
You will bring always a pleasant memory
Of all the good things that used to be.
We never used to think that we'd ever miss you:
Those laughing, joyful days were never blue.
You were the Mother we gave our all to,
You were the Father who'd gently subdue.
In you our fond hopes and ambitions grew;
Through you we added to the little we knew.

You bring poignant memories, some bitter, some sweet.
We learned to be wise, courteous and neat.
You pointed out the paths in which to guide our feet
You made our lives more full, more complete,
Learning to solve problems which in later life we'd meet.

Farewell, dear teachers, perhaps for the last,
Soon you and your books will be in the past.
When we are finally on life's waters cast
We'll look back and remember the chances by-passed.
There will be other chances in this world so vast—
Some will be slower and others be fast.

Farewell, dear classmates, so bright and gay;
From the narrow path may your feet never stray.
May you find joy and happiness all along life's way,
May you do not as we do, but as we say.
And as we leave you on that sad but glorious day,
When you think of us, may you always have something nice to say.

Farewell, Alma Mater, farewell to you,
We hope we shall always be faithful and true.
Those four years of our lives we gave to you,
May we look back on them and never feel blue
Even when wishing we were back there with you.

I Love Life—But

I've loved many people, family, friends;
Experienced much—such a wonderful life!
Beautiful trees, shimmering in the sunlight,
Sparkling in the snow, and even bare ones;
All the exquisite flowers—yet another tale!

I've cared for all the autos I've been privileged to drive,
And every delicious morsel I've been fortunate to ingest.
And books! Ah, yes! Enjoyed voraciously—
Written, collected, catalogued, discussed—
Outside of nature, the best gift God gave us.
I've appreciated without fail.

I've been here for quite a while
And, mostly, have loved it all.
And lest I forget—the fantastic art!
And music—lilting, soothing, happy, gay,
Something for every season and mood,
Chants, instrumentals, ballads, hymns and such,
Whining cowboys and hip-hop, not so much!

Yes, I've loved life and could list much more
Of that which I've enjoyed and even loved;
Dreams I've dreamed and visions I've seen,
Fantasies and fairy tales and songs God gave me,
Things I've imagined and those I can touch.

Yes, I love life, but can you even conceive—
Heaven will be even better than this!
Hallelujah!!!

"Taps" From a Distant Hill

As "Taps" was played from a distant hill
And echoed over the grave,
My mind and heart and soul stood still
But I saw the flag flutter and wave.

And then it was taken and carefully folded
And handed to one nearby,
Whose thoughts were locked in an icy grip,
Whose eyes refused to cry.
If only they could cry!

Those shiny medals—whatever they're made of—
Aren't very much to show
For the life of a valiant soldier
Who didn't really know

Just why he went off so far from home
And fought so hard, and died.
Who left his wife or folks or kids,
Or maybe a brand new bride.......Or did he?

If he could come back to answer us
Would he say that he'd do it again?
He must believe and so must we,
Or his death will have been in vain.
For centuries millions have fought and died,
And in future more millions will—
For God, for country, for honor, for pride,
And proud we must be of them still;
And feel a certain poignant thrill
As "Taps" is played from a distant hill.

Farewell, My Brother

Farewell, my brother, but not a final "goodbye".
I anticipate seeing you soon, one day across the sky—
That chasm that now separates you and I,
But we will meet again in Heaven by and by.

Farewell, my brother, you made my life a joy,
Though we sometimes differed, as any girl and boy,
I know, at times I could truly annoy
But at those times, your patience you'd employ.

It should not have been that way—
There should have been many more years for you to stay.
How were we to know there'd come a day
When you had to leave the earth and go away.

You've gone on ahead of me with no fear.
Many say "too soon", "too young"—but it's clear
That God had things for you to do down here,
But He loved and needed you there, my dear.

You will be missed, but I know there'll be a tomorrow
With no more knowledge of loss and of sorrow;
I feel your rejoicing up there above
As you prepare to receive those you love.

But only God knows when and how and why
And everything is in His time; and so "goodbye".
Goodbye, my brother, I will miss you, as I sigh,
And I can't help but wish that you didn't have to die.

Friends

Friends are responsible, even reliable;
Some are crazy—even certifiable!
They love to tell you all of their woes
From lovers to hangnails, ailments to clothes.
Friends are scarce, acquaintances many
The latter all turn up like a bad penny.
With some you can play and laugh and talk
But with your confidences you balk.
With a few you may be able to let down your hair,
To pour out your heart, your joy, your despair,
But some don't know when to keep it private.
Your business with them will never be quiet.
My life has been full of people—so many!
But few made the grade as friend, if any.
You try and you try, up to the very end;
You'll know the worth of a truly good friend!

For Her Family

A little bit weary, but humming, nonetheless,
Puttering around her kitchen, measuring, stirring, sifting,
Banging pots and pans: she's baking for her family;
And for her it's eminently uplifting!

Sweeping, dusting, scrubbing all the corners,
Cleanliness is next to Godliness is her creed,
Her greatest joy is making her house sparkle,
All for her family, and it fills a deep-seated need.

Chauffeuring, schlepping, whatever you may call it,
Grocery-shopping, taking children here and there,
Ever-going, ever-moving, seldom lighting in one place,
Always on the go, seemingly everywhere!

All for her family, she'll be the first to tell you.
For her Lord, and kids and husband always working;
Add stranger or friend into the mix, it will not faze her,
This is the life she's never, ever shirking!

What a paragon of virtue is the busy, happy Mother.
Even at the times when she gets aggravated
They are understandable and forgivable by everyone,
Because it's very clear her love has never dissipated.

Ike

My father's name was Ike.
He would never go on strike,
For the Union was anathema to him.
   He fed his family well,
   And as anyone could tell
His love for them never did grow dim.

He lived his life by a higher rule,
And certainly was nobody's fool,
But a victim of the time in which he was caught.
   He deemed his wife a perfect jewel,
   Definitely a man of the old school,
And so much happiness to our lives he brought.

What can you say about a Dad
Who really gave it all he had
But thought he always had to stay so tough?
   He worked until the day he died
   To be the best at all he tried,
Not realizing just being "Ike" would be enough.

Maude

"Spell it with an 'e' at the end," she said,
"Or it looks like mud."
A little girl dressed all in white,
With long white stockings to hide the skinned knees;
Long, black "baloney curls" tied with a bow,
And big, big, big brown laughing eyes.
I didn't know that little girl,
Or even the young woman;
I little knew the lovely mother she became
When I was born.
But well I remember her aura!
The feelings of love and security and being wanted!
Which is really what it's all about.
The sweetness and joy and humor
She shared with all who knew her.
It was said of her, "Maude never met an enemy".
Oh, I saw her angry when someone was mean or unkind
To her husband or children or friends.
And I saw her cry—when we cried.
And I saw her die—much before her time—or was it?
From her I learned about loving and living,
And if my life is lacking in someone's eyes,
Let it never be said Maude was to blame!
Coincidence her name's alliterative with Mother?
 Mary, Madonna, Maude?
 I think not!

Sometimes a Daughter

Sometimes a daughter can be so helpful.
Sometimes she can make you so very sad.
At times she's as sweet as a candy bar
And other times she makes you just plain mad!
One day she's little and helpless and fragile,
The next she's half grown and a royal pain!
Then before you can blink she's a woman
And the circle of life begins again.

Infant, toddler, pretty child,
Precocious teen—a little wild,
Smart, pretty—you're so very proud!
Prayerful lady with head bowed,
Lovely image of Madonna and child;
Loving, giving, courageous, mild,
Strong, valiant, never cowed—
    My Daughter

Rock My Baby Boy

Mother Mary, rock my baby boy;
You understand, because you lost your Son,
Not as a baby, but, worse, when He was fully grown!

I know God wants my baby there,
And he will be made so happy up in Heaven,
But my mother-heart just misses rocking him.

Mary, won't you hold him for me,
Rock him, cuddle him, smile at him for me,
And let him know I love him, now and forever.

Take my baby boy and watch him grow,
And train him up to be useful to the Lord,
And when I get there I will happily rejoice with him.

But for now, just rock my baby boy;
Maybe sing to him a lullaby, as I would have,
And surround him with the love he could not stay to see.

Mack

I called him Mack—now that's a pretty silly name,
Not Mike nor Mark nor even Mac, you see.
 I needed a one-of-a-kind, private nick-name
That was unique and only known to me.
A name that no one ever called him, or at least
A distinctive spelling variant, mine exclusively.

His name was Leon Sheridan Duane—oh, my!
What a terribly long handle for a little one.
As a child they called him Leon, mostly Lee,
Of course, they called him Brother, Kid and Son.
The kids, unkindly, Short-Stuff, Mo, and Skinny;
And then, Shorty, but Mac is what he did become.

But I always called him Mack—I was the only one
Who ever spelled it that way, and they thought me dumb;
Little did they know that it was very deliberate.
A pet name, if you will, understood by only some
Who knew that he was once my world to me,
Until, alas, that too-short time was done.

WAFs in a Weary World

WE are women—hear us roar!
  We are Air Force—watch us soar!
    Korea, Desert Storm, Viet Nam,
      We helped our country be "what it am".
Not just freeing men to do their thing,
  We were part of everything:
    Drill Instructor, teacher, veterinary tech,
      Food inspector, policeman—what the heck!
We have lots of hidden talents
  You didn't know about;
    But one thing we gave in common:
      We're very glad we're out!

Sleep, Little Baby

Lay your curly golden head
On your pillow so fragrant and sweet;
Fairies dance about your bed
And angels at your feet.

The sun is shining just for you,
The water's running deep;
The birds will hush their song for you
So you may go to sleep.

Leave the world to itself for now,
Give never a thought nor care;
For it must go on, anyhow—
When you awake it will be there.

Lie in your little bed of white,
Dream your golden dreams;
For you things will always be good and right
And you'll fulfill your schemes.

May you always be fortunate, little one,
Little pink baby of mine,
May your days always be as the shining sun,
And your life be good and fine.

To Be Me

I haven't been called to be pretty,
Or super spiritual or smart;
I don't have to be younger or older,
I just have to have heart.

I owe my Lord all my efforts
To be all that I can be.
Spiritually, mentally, physically,
I'm called to just be the best Me!

If I marry I owe my husband
To be as attractive as I can be
As supportive and loving and kind
Without any artificiality.

I must be true to myself,
Even if I should never remarry,
And remain loving and giving,
Not stiff and remote and starchy.

I will not be afraid to love
Wholly, heartily, completely;
Not searching for love in return,
Just accepting what He has for me.

I will remember that love is patient,
Long suffering, and does not boast—
Except of the Lord and His blessings
And that's what I love the most.

Love is never proud or arrogant,
Acting with common sense, becomingly;
Does not seek its own, nor easily provoked,
And learns to do what is required of me.

Seventy-two and Holding

Happy Birthday to me, Happy Birthday to me!
Even turning seventy-two is a big deal to me.
Imagine what I'll feel like when turning seventy-three!

My poor old ankle acts up once in a while,
My feet ain't as good as they used to be;
I feel on this day that I sure ain't no chile
My knees, hips and back they ain't dancey.

My nose ain't so bad, as noses go,
But it now has some scars I ain't showin',
My mouth still is turnin' up like a bow,
And my mind is definitely still growin'.

The old eyes need these panes to hide back of,
And even then they just don't do night;
But still I can read and drive up a storm,
And as long as I can, I'm all right!

At seventy-two I'm still sharp as a tack,
Though the point on the tack's a bit blunted;
My memories are keen and I know quite a bit
About a lot—'cause I've hunted.

Yep, my get up and go has got up and went,
And my "live-in" is old Arthur Ite Us;
But most of the time we don't fight too much,
He's much better than old Penn D'Citis!

I have 4 other friends in whom I delight:
Ben and Jerry and Baskin and Robbin;
I can't indulge with them too many times
As they're makin' me look like Old Dobbin.

I feel great and I'm happy and singing a song
As I continue completing my task;
I'm old but I'm free and still young in the Lord—
In that I will always bask.

Happy Birthday to me, Happy Birthday to me!
Join me in singing and being all we can be
To God, to each other, to me!

Diamond Jubilee

This is my Diamond Jubilee—
Seventy-five years that I've been me.
I never thought that I could be
A victim of such longevity.

Years ago, and they were many,
I figured I might last to age sixty-three;
But the closer I came to retire, you see,
I adjusted my timetable to age seventy-three.

Well, guess what? That's been done
So I think I'll shoot for eighty-one!
Or should my course not yet be run
I'll expect no less than ninety-one.

Perhaps I'll be having so much fun
That I will simply outlive everyone!
The thing I know is just this one:
I'll definitely stay till my work is done.

Fourscore

I now have something in common with Lincoln
And his Gettysburg Address:
I can finally claim the words "Fourscore".
It's been so long and yet so short,
It's been so little and yet "so more".

When I was young, fifty seemed so old.
It wasn't an age I thought I'd ever achieve;
But time marches on and so do birthdays
And when 60 arrived I was somewhat relieved.

After that it was all a blur:
70' and 80's were incomprehensible!
"Ill never get that old," I thought.
My arguments were indefensible.

Time and tide wait for no man.
Before I blinked twice—or maybe it was more—
I arrived at that which I once deemed impossible:
That previously unheard of . . ."Fourscore";
And God alone can tell if I'll get to 81 or more!

Mind Reader

When I read a book I'm astounded—
I second-guess the characters—it's so funny!
I seem to be able to predict what they'll do
And it's usually right on the money!

I think I am psychic, I know what they'll be doing,
I can tell just who will end up with who.
I'm impatient with all of the games they are playing;
Wish they'd cut to the chase, don't you?

As to my own family—I know what they should do,
And I know I'm almost always right.
Bill should definitely marry Karen,
And she shouldn't put up such a fight.

Daisy and Deborah should finish college
And not spend so much time with the boys;
My daughters should be much stricter mothers
And not put up with quite so much noise.

My grandson should be making more money,
I can see he's just not appreciated.
Always being on time and toadying up to the boss
Is actually much over-rated.

I see clearly they all could do better,
If only they'd heed their old mother.
Now long will it be till they listen to me
And ignore what they're told by another?

In people-watching it is much the same.
I can mostly tell where they're headed;
Which ones are hurrying off to a date
And which are blissfully wedded.

Which man's contemplating a nefarious deed
And how soon he will be apprehended?
There's that girl who is rushing quickly away
In tears, for the affair that has ended.

I am so good at this reading their minds
And the outcomes are just so "delish"—
I could easily become a very great prophet,
Knowing how it all ends—I wish!

You Are Blessed of God

Dad, you are blessed of God,
You've sired and raised a child.
Though that daughter may be a terror
And that son be terribly wild,
You've taught them and loved them
And nurtured and led.
The way's not always been smooth,
Sometimes you've even bled.

But you know God forgives *your* foibles
And rewards *your* success.
So with those children He gave you
You can certainly do no less!
Enjoy the blessings of *your* Father
And know that you've done your best.
God honors His men that are fathers:
Yes, Dad, you are truly blessed!

Healthy to Dead

Who'd a thought it? I'm seventy-five!
Never dreamed I'd still be alive.
Grammy died in her sleep at age 51
And Mom went to heaven at age 61.
Till the very end they seemed healthy.
Tho' neither was very wealthy;
I am not as well off as either,
Financially nor physically, neither.

Five more years or even more?
I can't conceive of what might be in store.
At times it seems to boggle my mind
To try to conjecture just what I will find;
A few more weeks, or months, or years,
Many more sorrows or numerous tears?
Or will it be, as many say,
That Jesus might come back today?

I can only dream of that possibility,
That very soon He'll come back for me.
I know He will come, just don't know when,
And find it hard to believe it's within my ken
To understand all the ramifications—
It's futile to imagine all the complications!
But come He will, and I will go
To forever be with Him—that I know.

Whether at the Rapture He comes for me,
Or before—a distinct possibility.
I know not how many years are before me,
Or what He has in store, don't you see?
Some insist we're allotted one-hundred-and-twenty
But however many I'm sure 'twill be plenty.
I pray in my heart, not in my head,
That He'll allow me to go straight from healthy to dead!

ON THE LIGHTER SIDE

Happy Camper

Growing old doesn't make me unhappy,
Getting older doesn't really make me sad;
But I miss the legs that used to run and jump
And moving nimble fingers would make me glad.

I don't miss driving my car everywhere
'Cross town or across countryside far;
But I sometimes miss the independence of it,
And I sometimes miss my car.

I miss the sharp eyes I used to enjoy—
Now I sometimes can't see across the street.
It's hard to grasp onto a pencil to write
And noting the color of your eyes would be sweet.

I raised my kids, and don't want to repeat it,
But remembering their hugs and kisses
And cuddling a baby close in my arms
Are the things that a mother misses.

I don't bewail that I'm no longer married,
Tho' close companionship is always nice;
I sometimes yearn for the company of a man,
And really miss the scent of "Old Spice".

Yes, there are things I often miss,
But they seldom put a damper
On all the lovely things I have and do.
All-in-all, I'm a Happy Camper!

Confused

I seem to have my days and nights confused—
Isn't that what's said of sleepless babes-in-arms?
Perhaps I'm in my second childhood now
And nothing really to raise such alarms.

I awaken often when I should be sleeping
And feel so sleepy when I want to be awake.
Perhaps a strategically taken sleeping pill
Would be the answer, for my sake.

Better yet, I think that I should just relax
And take the sleep—the not—whatever comes.
Perhaps it's best to just roll with the punches
And submit to whichever mode succumbs.

So I'll cease to be concerned about it;
I will surrender to the arms of Morpheus
Whenever that is what I'm feeling.
Whatever is the reason for such fuss?

I'll awake and be bright-eyed and bushy-tailed,
Alert and ready to go smell that lovely flower,
To do what I must do, or want to do, e'en tho'
I may be fast asleep again within the hour.

A Day in the Life of a Stapler

Push, push, click, click,
On and on it goes,
Fill it full as it can be.
Pound, pound, open, close,
Bind those books and
Clip those papers.
Never ending satisfaction,
Always cutting capers.
Staplers come in many colors,
Also come in black;
Taking a humongous chunk
Or just a little tack.
Ever present on my desk,
Always useful, always handy.
It's always fun to work with you:
You're just a little Dandy!

Every Two Hours

I live my life in increments, it seems.
Every two hours there's a different task.
One hour, then another one, or so,
I visit the facilities—don't ask!

I eat on approximately the same schedule,
I even sleep the same two hours, give or take.
Computering is very sleep inducing:
After 120 minutes I cannot stay awake.

I read about two hours at a time,
And only work full-out about the same.
So everything I do takes just two hours,
But, what the heck, that's how I play the game.

Dear Son

I'm behind in my writing,
So I thought I'd drop a line.
Don't worry about a thing here—
Copasetic down the line!

Your sister doesn't live here now—
She ran away last week.
She's living in a two room trailer
Down by Murray Creek.
The kitchen ceiling just fell down
When the bathroom sprung a leak.

Your brother broke his leg again—
The second time this year.
I'm finally losing weight at last
(The cost of food's so dear).
Your father's car was totaled,
But he's recovering, I hear.

But don't you worry 'bout a thing—
Not even brother Tom—
There wasn't too much damage done,
It was just a little bomb.
We're really doing great here.
(Signed) Your loving Mom.

Dessert Fixation

I have no one to bake for anymore
No one to bring all those tasty sweets.
So many times a day I think of something
To tempt you in the way of "eats".

You loved your goodies oh, so well,
And those who knew that, as I,
Knew that even when you couldn't eat your supper
You would always have room for pumpkin pie;

We'd bring you deserts (without the nuts)
To tempt your flagging appetite,
And bake you breads and pies and cakes
To fix you up just right!

I think that where you are right now
Is a great sugary smorgasbord
Prepared with all those special treats
That now you're sharing with the Lord!

Job's Sister

The coffee is bitter,
The tea's tasting....tannic?
Or maybe it's the sugar
I'm not supposed to have.
I'll never eat another egg—
`Without salt it has no taste at all.
My eyes are blurred,
Someone stuck a finger in my eye;
My knee zigs when I want to zag,
My feet are large and fat and puffy;
My mind is racing everywhere
But on what it's supposed to be concentrating.
My fingers hurt and lock,
They barely write a word.
My heart is no doubt beating fast,
But I can't see all of that.
But no boils or warts or lesions!
Oh, my, I've once again been reading "Job"
And identifying with his plight!
I'm really fine! And as he said:
"I will arise again as pure gold." (Job 23:10)

Every Other Day

Sometimes I think I live just every other day:
One day I take ALL my vitamin supplements,
Complete my Bible reading for the day,
Work my allotted hours on the computer,
Take my daily walk, eat my breakfast,
Accomplish something in or out of the house.
The next day I loll—sleep late, skip breakfast,
Ignore all the other things that I should do,
And read and rest and watch the idiot box—
And usually snack too much.
I need a goal to get up in the morning.
I need a "project" that I can sink my teeth into;
But I have three projects I could be working on,
And still……..

What would it take to change?
To be my so-called "old self"?
A paycheck at the completion of a project?
An "attagirl" from someone I admire?
Someone to admire?
Is it physical, mental or spiritual—
Or something of all three?
Activity begets activity,
Slothfulness begets fatigue and illness,
Depression makes one "blue".

I need to live all my days to the fullest,
Not skipping them for no reason at all.

Lists

I sit here in my chair making list after list
Of things to do and things I'd like to do;
Tasks I really need to accomplish
And probably I will
But it will take me 10 times longer
Than once it used to do.
I make out endless grocery lists
And stuff to buy some day,
And lists of what I want to do
When I have the time and the money,
And lists of those to call and see
Whenever I get the energy.
If I spent the same amount of time
Doing these things instead of making lists
Everything on my To Do list
Would already have been Ta-Done!

Water Bottle World

Everywhere I go
It's a "water-bottle-world"!
Up or down or left or right
Or whether "boyd" or girld"!
Indigent or yuppie,
Straight-haired or curled,
It's a water-bottle world.
It doesn't say much for the water
But a positive spin on our health;
It's good to hydrate the body,
Even if it doesn't add to our wealth.
Some entrepreneur from the country
Is getting rich on the concept.
But the idea of bottling water
Is not a secret well-kept.
You see it throughout the country,
The majority in the big city;
Now they're adding flavors
So it's no longer pure, more's the pity.

A Love Song

How do I love thee? Let me count the ways.
Yes, I know it's been done before, and better than I can do,
But you're all I seem to think about these days;
You make me happy when I'm down and blue.
When things go wrong you make them feel right,
When others forsake me you're here for me.
When I'm tired and lonely, early morning, late at night,
You're always sitting there waiting so patiently.
When I turn you on you light up my life!
You gurgle and whirr and purr and beep—
You're more interesting than husband—
You respond to my touch even half asleep;
As my fingers caress you, your response is immediate,
And way beyond my wildest expectation.
Your ease in handling is one key ingredient
In our relationship, and upon close examination,
It's so terribly convenient.
When I finally turn you off, there's no recriminations—
I leave with the complete assurance you'll remain
And be here awaiting my return, whenever I decide—
No matter how long it takes to come back to your side,
Once again running my hungry fingers up and down
Your smooth and lovely keyboard, watching your beautiful
Colors brightening my soul.
I can again pour out my heart to you, assured you will
Never relay it, betray it or delay my response to you.
How do I love thee? Many, many, many ways!
Every day you get more comfortable and cuter!
(If the guy that liked "Ben" can write a love song to a rat,
Then I can write a love song to my computer!)

Ode to an Egg

Kudos and praises for the egg incredible!
It makes my mouth smile and my taste buds sing.
All hail to thee, egg that's so edible,
What joy to all my senses you bring.

As I dip that tasty morsel of toasted bread
Into that yellow, tantalizing orb,
I know that I must so lightly tread
As I so efficiently my appetite curb.

I relish those bright, fluffy mounds of gold,
Scrambled so lightly, with just the right seasoning;
It's the food of the gods—or so I've been told—
And that's not at all beyond my mortal reasoning.

Oh, that soft, luscious flavor of the marvelous egg
Makes my morning or even my evening so nice.
Add some bacon and toast, I sometimes beg,
And my meal is complete; but just an egg would suffice.

All that I yearn for in culinary delight
Is the taste of an egg, scrambled, boiled or fried.
I can eat them morning, noon or night
And not tire of them, even if I tried.

Puzzle Meister

I have plenty to do, but still I sit
Wracking my brains making puzzles.
Big ones, little—tho' the latter not so much
Even one about a gown that rustles.
All kind of topics, stretching my brain here,
Really using all my imagination,
Searching the Internet for subjects
And deciding on the very pagination.
Bible Word Search: countries, states,
Sometimes the subject's obscure destinations.
Plants and movies, flowers and holidays,
And animals that require muzzles;
Nothing is beyond the scope
Of subject for all of my puzzles.
Why waste my time doing these things?
Perhaps I simply need to show that I can do
Puzzles that others want to solve and
Something that another might find difficult to do.
Don't know why I enjoy so making puzzles
If it was easy I wouldn't want to do it.
Perhaps you'd say this is the height of boredom—
Oh yeah? So go on and try it!

I Love Mondays

I love Mondays, don't you?
Or maybe not, since some people do
Seem to think that Mondays are blue.
But if you'd come to think of it as I do,
You might come to love Mondays, too.
That's not the first day of the week, it's true
But it's the start of the work-week I knew,
And a stupendous chance to start out anew,
Doing the things that you've wanted to do.
A beginning is great, it's brand-spanking new!
So how can a Monday still make you feel blue?
It's filled with new chances just lying in lieu
And the old junk you can simply toss in the loo!
So put on a big smile, and agree with me, do:
That I still love Mondays, and so should you.

Hurry!

You certainly can't hurry in a wheelchair,
You indubitably can't run with a cane,
You cannot rush about with a walker,
To endeavor to do so would be insane.
Perhaps in a power chair you can manage
To hurry just a little. You might gain
A few more steps than with a walker
But then you're back to square one again.
But thinking you can hurry when you can't
Is absolutely, positively inane.
It's important to remember at this stage of life
That slow and steady is the name of the game.

Maternity Myths

It's a myth about "eating for two",
And if I drink any more milk I'll begin to moo.
You want to kill the man who got you into this mess,
Finding out how you got here is anyone's guess.

Cravings aren't the least bit funny:
Dill pickles and hot sausage, and more;
Watermelon in the middle of the winter,
Ice cold beer when you never drank before;

Crying for no apparent reason,
Going from blues to Hallelujahs at the drop of a hat,
Or maybe the "screaming meemies"—
What's up with that?

They say a lady doesn't sweat, she glows.
What a crock! She sweats like a pig
From carrying all that weight around
And just from being so gol-durned big!

Maternity dresses are pretty—not!
Nowadays the dress for moms-to-be
Is skin-tight fashions that accentuate their size.
Anyone here that thinks that's so lovely?

But, anyway some of what they say is true:
At that Grand Finale, when you hear that first squall,
No matter what's gone before it,
It's been worth it all!

On Shopping

Who woulda thunk, at my advanced years,
That now I live to go shopping?
Whether or not I have the dinero
I love to go out just shopping

When I was young, when everyone else
Seemed to live to shop and spend,
I considered it a waste of time for me,
A bore, a chore, a dead end.

'Course then I was busy raising a husband
And umpty-eleven kids,
And hadn't the wherewithal to buy much—
Except when I had to, I did.

The styles just didn't interest me,
The shoes always pinched my big toe,
And nobody cared much, the clothes that I wore,
For there weren't many places to go.

Between no time, no money, no interest,
It wasn't much fun to go shopping;
Except for the few times I shopped with Mom,
But that was less about shopping than stopping.

Pick up a hankie or white shoe laces,
Then stop for a cup of coffee.
Perhaps we'd buy a dress or two,
Then to the candy shop for toffee.

Of course there was some window shopping.
Even not liking shopping, I dreamed
Of the day when shopping was not a big deal,
And life wasn't as bleak as it seemed.

But it was mostly the coffee and *all* about talking
'Cause she was a friend like no other.
Going shopping with her was not boring, you see.
She was a pal, my buddy, my Mother.

But that's not about which I'm writing here,
I'm relating the tale of how my life changed
From hating to loving the shopping experience—
That's how my days have been rearranged

Oh, yes, you can say that I'm old now,
And probably somewhat out of my gourd,
But it's really not true that I'm so blue
Or that I am exceedingly bored.

I just love to shop—that's it in a nutshell!
Although I don't "shop till I drop".
'Cause I "drop" quite often, 'neath a big, shady tree
But after a while I continue to shop.

And nowadays it's not shopping for clothing,
Or the big things that one usually sees,
But the little "junk shopping" or shopping for books,
Or—ready for this? Buying groceries!

Yes, I'm addicted to grocery and drug stores,
And those "all-purpose mega stores"—Wow!
I could spend my kids' inheritance there,
And beginning to do so right now!

My Red

I wrote a book about my Red—
Talking to him and such—
But nowhere in it does it say
That I loved him so much.

I sleep with him and hold him
Cuddled to my breast.
It is the greatest relationship—
He is definitely the best!

He listens to my every woe,
And dries my every tear;
Just talking things out with him
Makes everything so clear.

He never, ever says much,
He never eats my food,
He's always calm and quiet
And perpetually good!

He is continually my best friend,
He never goes away.
He's the one thing I can count on,
At the end of every day.

My Red is such a comfort
Even when I'm sleeping like a log.
He's forever there for me—
Red, my big stuffed dog!

On Aging

Do I sometimes look down upon aging ones?
They seem so fragile, even brittle.
Their tread has slowed, perhaps their speech.
Most of them appear so ————little!
As if not worth the time it takes
To wipe away their spittle.
Subconsciously, I consider myself
Only slightly less than my former self.
Ah, life is truly a riddle!

But, I too, am old, I just don't see it;
At times I still feel I can walk a mile.
Sometimes, in my mind, I am hale and hearty—
Still have the old panache, the style,
The old dreams and yearnings still remain,
Just buried deeply in my "pending" file.
I find myself planning my wedding dress,
My intended surely will be the best.
Why not? It makes me smile.

If we all truly felt the way we look
A sorrier sight you'd seldom see.
If we always looked the way we feel
We'd all certainly wallow in misery.
But the outer façade is always deceptive,
And feeling not necessarily how we will be.
We smile, we flirt,
Though we're older than dirt,
We—I—need to feel someone smiling at me.

Dreams die hard when you're up in years;
Some are still planning for a new house or car.
E'en though we're aware we couldn't care for them,
And the old eyes just don't see that far.
But life's all about dreaming, and planning, too:
When our goals are gone, there goes the last star.
So before we go into our proverbial holes,
We'll just learn to set some realistic goals
And latch onto the dreams our old lives can't mar.

Push Button World

I'm living in a push button world—
Who would ever have thought it?
Push PLAY to turn the music on,
Push REPEAT to keep it going;
STOP, START, FORWARD, SKIP,
There is one for everything!
There's a button to turn the coffee on,
And one to set the clock;
There's buttons for the microwave,
And, of course, one for the oven.
Never mind all the buttons on
Your cell phone—that's a given!
And the ones to control the DVD,
And more on the TV remote
Than I shall ever use, believe me.
There are buttons on my blouses—
Too bad there's none to cook for me,
Or ones to clean our houses.
But now, here's the absolute kicker—
It will really mess up your head—
It's the icing on your chocolate cake—
I now have a push button bed!

Motel Mentality

Hotel, Motel, Travel, Refugee—
Whatever you want to call it—
It's the mindset one gets
When traveling or staying overnight:
I am locked in for the night!
I can't get any more food!
I must stock up now
For I may never eat again!
Of course my car is just outside,
And, of course, I've got two feet,
But somehow I am reticent to
Venture out at night
In an unknown, unfamiliar town
Or even dressing again.
No, it's not very logical,
In fact, it's really bizarre,
But that Motel Mentality
Grabs at my mind tenaciously
And doesn't want to let go.

LOVE MAKES THE WORLD GO 'ROUND

Awake Little Flower

Awake, little flower, little yellow buttercup,
Smile at the golden sun;
Every little leaf and bud, wake up,
Tell him it's he and only he
That now I love and always will.
Our love will last until eternity,
When the earth exists no more I'll love him still.

They told me love was only for the blind,
And once I thought that they were right.
I tried so hard for true love to find,
And failed, and thought at last I'd seen the light.
But then, one day, someone came along
Who took my life and turned it upside down.
He took my heart and filled it with a song,
My resolutions tumbled to the ground.

Now I can speak of love like any other,
Now my heart, too, can sing its gay love song.
My love is real, there'll never be another;
We'll always be together, right or wrong.
Awake, little flower, little yellow buttercup,
Smile at the golden summer sun,
Smile at my one and only one.

I Love You

Lovers have a vocabulary all their very own
But the words have been said so often that they're worn;
I want to whisper love words meant for you alone,
   To tell you of a new love
   A tried and true love,
To make you understand the way I feel.

I'd tell you of the feeling when I hold your hand,
And the way my heart leaps at your step.
   To tell you what it's like to talk
   And know you understand—
To know you understand the words unsaid.

I'd whisper of sensations when your lips meet mine
And how my body trembles at your touch.
I'd say that you mean more to me than life,
   And how it feels to be a wife,
   To share the joys of life
But most of all the sorrows and the strife.

And whene'er you go away
My small world tumbles down,
My sunny skies all turn to gray,
And living's not worthwhile.
   But knowing you'll return some day
   Keeps hope aflame—but such a small flame!
Thank God, when nothing's left I still can pray.

I pray for you each morning and each night,
I pray that He will guard you and protect you,
And help you know the wrong from right,
Your health and happiness mean more than anything
   And selfishly, at the end I pray
   You'll grow to love me
More and more with each passing day.

Help me try to say what I must say to you,
All this and much, much more,
For words are insufficient to articulate my love,
It's too strong a feeling to be inadequately expressed.
  I pray God you will know just what I mean
    When, trembling, unsure,
      Except of what I need to say.
        I whisper simply . . . I love you.

Enthusiastic Lover

I want to be an enthusiastic lover!
Deep inside I know that I really am.
I want to love someone who enjoys
My touching even in a not-so-private setting;
I want to feel free to hold his hand in public,
Perhaps even kiss him on the cheek;
I want to hug and be hugged
Whenever the urge arises—
Not in an inappropriate manner—
I am, after all, a lady.
But I want to be an enthusiastic lover;
To feel free to show the world that he's my man.
I want to love him, no holds barred,
Passionately, vociferously, enthusiastically!
I never did. I never could. I know now I never will.
That's so sad........I had so much love to give.

I Love Him Still

We will never experience "married love",
We will never ever be lovers,
But we'll always have God's love,
And such sweet memories.

I can't even see him now,
And wouldn't if I could;
He's "taken" now, but still, somehow,
Poor fool that I am, I love him still.

I'll Go on without You

I'll go on without you
  I'll go on as I did before.
Although my heart is breaking,
For it's you I'm longing for.

I'll go on without you
  Tho' my heart is breaking in two,
There's nothing left to say or do,
  I'll go on as you'd want me to.

I'll go on without you,
  For in God I've put my trust.
I'll go on without you,
  But only if I must.

I told you that I loved you,
And you said you loved me, too;
So now there's only one thing to do—
Pray to be half good enough for you.

If I should go to heaven
I know you'll be there, too.
Then dear, I'll come to you.
For darling, then I'll be—
  And only then I'll be—
    Half good enough for you,

Flowers and Fantasies

I can enjoy the little tokens, the occasional luncheons
The glances, the flowers, and the fantasies;
I can dream my dreams in my bed at night,
But each time it brings me to my knees
Because that's all the farther it will go.
It titillates, the thoughts of a relationship,
It's been such a long time since someone's come along;
It helps me feel better about myself and makes me smile,
I sometimes feel like breaking into song,
But I know that nothing will come of it.

I know that I should nip it in the bud, as it were
But it's a delight to indulge my imagination.
I love that there's still someone out there who loves me!
I want it to last, even if it's of short duration.
Even if it's not going anywhere.
No one is really being hurt by it—
I believe I can do it without repercussions.
So, in the meantime, I'll try it.
Although I know it is all a dead end.

I know I am vulnerable, my emotions so fragile
I have a tendency to laugh a lot and sometimes cry;
I whirl about on an out-of-control merry-go-round;
Often I'm laughing, just as often I sigh.
When will this phase of my life be over?
Someone once wrote, "Youth is wasted on the young".
It's not so, I've found—I was smarter back then!
But the patterns of the past keep repeating themselves.
And unrequited love rears its ugly head—again
And I find I'm really no smarter at all.
I thought I could just enjoy the chaste kisses
And gaze at his roses and smile;
I kept telling myself it wouldn't hurt anybody,
We could keep on being good friends for a while.
Then why is my conscience so burdened?
As sweet and as innocent as it continues to be,
I've finally realized what I've become—
The woman I've always despised,
The one who didn't have sense enough to run!
There's only one out for temptation—to flee

Angels

Do you believe in angels? You know that I do.
I know you're an angel. God sent me you.
He touched you with color and sweetness and light
And all that is goodness and all that is right.
It wasn't romantic, yet much more than a friend.
You and I have a bond forged on past the end.
When others are romping around on their clouds
We'll have something special, apart from the crowds.
It's friendship that's hewn from the Rock of Ages.
A love unexplainable upon these pages.
I know you're an angel from heaven above.
I know you're someone God gave me to love.

Gift of Love

Do you have the great gift for loving—
One that needs to be brought forth and used,
Not stored within a keepsake box
Where memories are kept to be mused
Upon and remembered and treasured
But never brought out to be abused?
A gift like that is meant to be shared.
That's especially true of the gift of love.
Those with the gift for loving
Are few and far between, it seems,
And some of those never use their gift
For anything but fulfilling their own dreams.

Pain and hurts, unrequited affection,
Can cause love to be bound
In a box or an air-tight chamber,
With no other emotions around.

We guard our emotions as if they were jewels
And hide them away where they can't be found.
But that is not what it's made for,
That is not its ultimate place.

The gift of loving must be used,
Not just to procreate the human race,
But to bring itself to full fruition
And to gaze upon a lover's face.

Don't close up your gift in a treasure chest
And put away the key.
Open it and use it to the fullest
Through all eternity.
Perhaps you are already beginning to—
Dare I pray you will give it to me?

There's No Fool Like an Old Fool

There's no fool like an old fool,
Of women or of men that's essentially true.
At least when it comes to infatuation,
It seems that's not true for just a few.

The need for love and romance doesn't leave us
Just because the bones are creaky and the hair is white;
Flippantly we say, "been there, done that"
When all the time we long for some "that" in sight.

How can a supposedly mature person
Exist on such a pittance of romance?
A twelve-year-old knows there really should be more
Than an occasional word or an amorous glance.

But everyone is sometimes prone to be a fool,
Though young or old or somewhere in between.
And I wouldn't really have it any other way.
I'll stay a fool for a sweet, romantic scene!

Half Good Enough

If I deserved somebody
Just half as good as you,
Then maybe I could hope to be
Half good enough for you.

There's no one in the universe
That can compare with you;
There's no one in this world of ours
That's half so fine and true.

If I deserved somebody
Half as wonderful as you,
Then someday I might hope to be
Half good enough for you.

Don't Ever Lose Your Sunny Smile

Don't ever lose your sunny smile,
Don't ever lose the sparkle in your eyes;
Don't ever lose the lilt in your laughter,
Or the blue will fade from the skies.

Don't ever lose the dimple in your cheek,
Don't ever lose the song in your heart
Don't ever lose the spring in your step,
Or this old world will fall apart.

You may go far away,
You may even go to stay,
There's nothing I can say,
But please listen as I pray.

Don't ever lose your sunny smile,
For that's what makes living worthwhile.
So no matter what you do, remember all the while
Don't ever lose your sunny smile.

Sing a Song to My Beloved

Sing a song to my beloved,
Sing a song to him today;
Keep a record of the songs you sing,
Keep a record of the things you say.

Sing a song to my beloved,
Sing it soft and sweet and low;
Tell him all the things I cannot,
Tell him that I love him so.

Sing of stars that lose their splendor
When he's gone away from me;
Sing of wind no longer tender
When it's not caressing him.

Sing a song to my beloved
While the moon sails high above.
Tell him that my heart is true,
And it's he I'll always love.

Special Friend

I had a special friend that I loved so very much,
But God had something else planned for our lives.
It is sometimes hard to know what He is planning,
Especially when you are so busy "running ahead of Him".

We meant to much to each other—such great friends.
We spent many sweet and pleasant hours
Sharing thoughts, ambitions and dreams,
Until we seemed to know one another intimately.

I loved the way he looked, his eyes, his sense of humor,
His sweetness and gentleness, especially with children.
Everyone spoke of his kindness and compassion.
How I loved to hear him sing and praise the Lord!

There are so many memories I have of my special friend.
Sweet and funny and sorrowful and poignant.
But the greatest thing I will always love about him
Is how he loved the Lord!

You Needn't Say You Love Me

When we're making love you needn't say you love me,
You needn't hold me tightly when we dance;
Don't laugh at all my jokes, they just aren't funny;
You're not obligated to speak words of romance,
You never have to say the word "forever"
I'll just assume it's there and take the chance.

The words won't matter to me if you're near me;
I won't ask anything of you on your part;
Inside I'll be imagining all those whispers,
Although I know it certainly isn't smart.
I'll feel all the tender words you aren't saying:
Fool that I am, I'll say them for you in my heart.

Crazy, Mixed-up World

It's a crazy, mixed-up world we live in,
Full of trouble, care and strife,
But a pretty good world in which to be
When I love you and you love me.

Two crazy people is what we are,
Pinning our hopes on a falling star;
Two little dopes who thing they're in love—
Maybe we're just in love with love.

I wish I could tell you how I feel—
It's a feeling that seems strange, yet real;
Please tell me, dear, just what to do,
And why I'm so much in love with you.

The grass is greener, the sky so blue
Whenever I get a letter from you;
But I can't hold a letter in my arms
And guide and protect it from all harms.

There's so much that I'd like to say
And so much more I'd like to do,
But all I ever seem to say
Is, "Darling, I love you".

It's a crazy, mixed-up world we're in—
Everything's backward and upside down.
I'm oblivious to pain and care and sin,
My head is spinning 'round and 'round.

We're as crazy as two people can be,
Walking in circles, with heads in the air.
All I know is I love you and you love me,
And that's all I want or hope for or care.

Only Let Me Love You

Only let me love you
For a little while;
Only let me love you,
Let me hold your hand and see you smile.

My darling, please be fair;
For you I'll always yearn.
Only let me care
And I'll ask nothing in return.

Is it asking too much
For me to ask for one more chance,
Is it *too* much
To ask to prove it's not just romance?

I've been searching for
Someone to adore,
And I have found that in you.
So only let me love you.

Only let me love you,
Darling, hear my plea
Only let me love you
Till the end of eternity.

Pocket

I don't want to live in your pocket,
I don't want you to live in mine.
I like it just the way it is.
Stay that way, it will be fine.

But sometimes—just sometimes—that pocket
Seems like a marvelous thing.
It's warm and cozy, enveloped in love,
And the closeness that true love can bring.

Sometimes a body needs holding,
Whether in a pocket or not;
One needs a tender touch to show love,
And a gentle finger a tear to blot.

Perhaps I'm not so independent
And neither, my dear, are you.
Let's rethink the subject of pockets,
But enlarged to accommodate two!

Shine Golden Sun

Shine golden sun, upon my love;
Send down your rays to kiss him.
Sparkle, cool water, around my love,
Stretch out your arms to embrace him.
Sing little birds, sing to my love,
Sing sweetly and softly and low,
Whisper warm breeze to my love;
Tell him I love him so.

Still Dreaming

Do you keep on dreaming
When you're past "the age of reason"?
Do you entertain thoughts of romance
When it is long past your "season"?
Are romantic songs and poems
Just there for the teasin'?

Do the moonlight and love scenes
Stir you down to your toes?
Does warm and dreamy ambience
Make you forget all your woes,
As you fantasize and daydream
Of dark and dashing heroes? Yes!

Sweet Times

There comes a time when you no longer remember
The sweet times, the pleasant times,
The cuddling-up-together times—
There surely must have been such times!
But now I can no longer recall
That there were any of those times.

There must have been a time
We laughed and talked together;
There must have been a day
We mentioned more than just the weather.

There must have been occasions that
He looked at me and held my hand,
When he'd gaze into my eyes
And I thought he'd understand.

There surely were those times
We held each other and felt that life was good;
When we knew we'd always be together—
Foolishly, I really thought we would!

I long to remember what has been forgotten.
Memory is capricious, at its best;
But, sadly, no remembrance of the sweet times.
I recall just the traumatic, not the rest.

Yearning

I've not given up hope to find someone to love me—
As humans, it's part of our DNA.
I am not needy, or desperate or even expectant,
Simply open to the possibility, as they say.

I'm exceedingly aware of my limitations,
Handicaps, foibles and just reasons why
There's not much of a chance to ever find someone
To love and to cherish me until I die.

Nevertheless, I remain open-minded,
Or perhaps open-hearted is the right word.
It's innate in us all to strive for completion,
And a special relationship strikes the right chord.

If there is someone out there made for me,
The other half of myself I am needing,
Please send him my way or take the yearning away,
And cease this ridiculous pleading.

Philosophical Question

What is love, anyway? Carnal love at least;
It comes, it goes, it passes or it stays.
We love so many people in our lives
To forget, or remember all our days.

Funny—the bad loves we remember
And the sweet ones we too soon forget;
Perhaps because the former are traumatic
The latter we too often must forfeit.

It is probably a philosophical question
That is certainly worthy of debate.
That those in our lives we most think of
Are the people that we most hate.

Oh, we don't hate anyone, you say;
Well, perhaps we just hate the deeds.
The times when we were lost and hurt
And that no one fulfilled our needs.

I'd like to recall just the sweet times,
The wonderful people I've met;
The fascinating conversations we've had
So fortunate to meet téte a téte.

Alas! I recall most the others;
The disparagement, the lies, the embarrassment,
The ones that didn't seem to like me
Those whose joy was my harassment.

I'm so blessed to have had those good times
And relatively few of the other kind,
So why think of those poor pitiful people
When I can bring all the others to mind?

So what is love, anyway? I don't know.
It would merely be conjecture on my part.
To say definitely what it is or isn't
It's too futile to endeavor to start!

Walking and Talking

It's a beautiful morning to take a walk,
What a marvelous way for us to talk
What a wonderful plan
For two to be together;
Walking and talking in the sun,
Don't have to hurry,
Don't have to run,
Even in inclement weather.
Walking along and having fun,
Laughing with that special someone,
Whisp'ring sweet nothings in her ear,
Softly, sweetly, no one can hear;
Vowing anew to leave her never.
What a beautiful day to walk along,
Softly humming your favorite song,
If life could only go on like this forever!

HAPPIEST TIME OF THE YEAR

Thanksgiving Dinner

Turkeys roasting,
Biscuits toasting,
Thanksgiving Day is really here!

Ovens warming,
Children swarming,
Making so much noise no one can hear!

Pots brewing,
Apples stewing,
There's never a second in which to brood.

Soups boiling,
Cooks toiling,
Just smell the delicious aroma of food!

Kettles simmering,
Eyes glimmering,
With thoughts of a Thanksgiving Dinner so gay.

So let's all pray,
And give thanks today,
(And for the Thanksgiving Dinner, let's shout, "hurray"!)

Anticipation of Christmas

I can't write a poem on the subject
Because there's just too much to say
About anticipating the season
That leads up to Christmas Day.

Sometimes I begin as early as October,
Every year I decorate earlier; I find
The anticipation starts to boil and stir
Until I just can't get it out of my mind.

Suddenly the time-line's quickly shortened,
The mind kick-starts the body into high gear.
Nothing like anticipation to fire up the body.
Now you're fast-approaching that New Year.

I plan it now to include everything I like
While also making room for contemplation.
The best part of it all is sitting back to savor
The marvelous and wonderful sensations.

I love to listen to all the songs and carols,
I love to watch the Christmas lights—
The colors winking on my tree
Brighten up my night and fill me with delight.

All my kitchen's aromatic scents
That telegraph all the Christmas baking,
And that, as we get up in years,
Is quite an undertaking.

Still I endeavor to do whate'er I can
To prepare a luscious holiday treat;
Not the quantity of former years,
But even a few, for me is quite a feat.

Ah, Christmas—or is it just the anticipation
That makes me crazy and yet so joyful?
My internal motor stays on overdrive!
It's frenetic, insane, and yet so beautiful!

No wonder we "fall apart" the day after!
Or as I have stated, I say in summation,
It's not really the day
But the anticipation!

My Christmas

The glowing star atop the shiny tree,
The glittering lights and the ornaments you see,
    Are not my Christmas.

The food, the friends, the frolicking in the snow,
The joyous camaraderie everywhere you go,
    Are not my Christmas.

All the decorations, lovely as they are,
From the tiniest angel to the shiniest star,
    These are not my Christmas.

There are packages galore underneath the branches,
The least amount of movement causes avalanches.
    That is not my Christmas.

Then melodies of carolers upon a Christmas Eve,
So marvelous these songs, one *cannot* grieve.
    But these are not my Christmas.

Such wonderful memories of Christmases past,
And the joy and the peace and the love that will last,
    But still, that's not my Christmas,

Even the Manger Scenes—Holy Mary, meek and mild,
Manly Joseph and the precious Infant Child—
    Now it's closer to my Christmas,

Without any of the things above,
Even without family or friends, or even love,
I would still have Christmas.
    For Christmas is Jesus
    And Jesus is my Christmas!

That Christmas Feeling

I love to watch the candles flicker and flame,
Sending out their whiffs of spicy pine.
It's almost like Christmas
And that's a favorite time of mine.

I love to see the first lights on the streets
Turn on way ahead of time,
But never too soon for me;
Even in July, to me, would be just fine.

To feel that it is Christmas time
One doesn't need the sight of snow,
Just a certain scent in the air
That triggers the remembrance of snow.

The sights, the sounds, the memories
Of holidays so long ago.
Even living deeply in the South—
It's foolish—but it smells like snow!

But it is more the ambience,
The accumulation of the years
And gifts and givers,
Remembering laughs and tears.

Past and present—and the presents!
No, it's not that either.
It's all of the above and more
And yet it is neither.

It's a certain Christmas feeling
That comes over me unaware.
I'm seldom anticipating it
But sometimes it's just there.

Something extraordinary,
Something very sweet and rare;
An old-fashioned word today,
But it really feels quite quare.

I'll watch the shops gear up for
Their favorite holiday—and mine.
I'll plunge in deep
  With both my feet
    And not much sleep
But great enthusiasm for the time!

I yet can be mentally excited
When my vitality winds down,
When my energy's depleted
Till my "to-do-list" is completed,
Still I'll think of something else to do
Until the Big Day is repleted.

Christmas may be a frenetic time
And yet it is a time of peace.
It's a season of hustle and bustle
Yet a season for strife to cease.

In the midst of all the trimmings
I enjoy the calm and serene.
The spectacular holiday tree,
The simplicity of pure, white snow.
From the sublime to the ridiculous
And everywhere in between.

It's a time of lows and a time of highs,
Peaks and valleys and flat-line spaces
Just to "chill-out" and get your bearings,
To relish the hugs and embraces,
To rejoice in all the people and things
And all the Christmas-kissed places.

Yes, I love that Christmas feeling,
Though ephemeral and fleeting;
Even the briefest moment in time
Is worth the quickest meeting.
If you can catch that wee small moment
It will start your heart to beating
And cause you to reflect on
A special Christmas greeting.

Christmas Season

It's another Christmas Season,
Another Christmas night.
Parties to be planning,
Gifts furtively pushed out of sight.
It may be different this year,
But it still will be all right.

The cherished Christmas ornaments
Are once again in place,
The colored lights, the holly,
But missing is the frenzied pace.
No more pushing, prodding, scheming,
No more Christmas-time rat-race.

Everything is changing,
No more status quo.
Yes, every year is different,
But that is how we grow.
One just rolls with the punches,
It's a new year, don't you know?

We must embrace the new time,
Traditions are sometimes made to be broken.
But the tradition of love and of family
Is always much more than a token
Of all we remember and care for
In all the sweet words we have spoken.

As families increase and decrease
It's the ebb and flow of life;
We enjoy the one time all year
That seems to be free of strife;
The warmth between siblings and offspring,
And even estranged husband and wife.

It's yet another Christmas Season,
And the world seems to be so right.
Enmity is pushed aside for a time
And we forget the woes and plight,
When we concentrate on the Season
And that glorious Christmas Night.

Oh, the beautiful Christmas Season,
Ever-changing yet somehow the same;
If we can't feel the wonder of Christmas
We have only ourselves to blame.
It's always different, yes that's true,
But still when Jesus came!

Christmas Is a Promise

Christmas is a promise coming true
Of everything you've dreamed of, longed for, hoped for;
A nebulous, intangible, can't-put-your-finger-on-it
Yearning desire for something more;
And if I should happen to shed a wee tear
At the height of the Christmas festivities,
It's because I'm just a sentimental fool
And always will be, if you please!

Christmas Reverie

I'm lying here flat on my back
Watching the few Christmas lights
I've managed to string before "the fall".
The pain in my knees is giving me fits
But the house is decorated up all right.
Who needs a tinselly tree at all?

I'm down to my last six-fifty or so,
But most of the gifts are all bought,
And out of a hundred, ten cards are sent.
I'm going through tissues like they're going out of style
Thanks to this cold that I've caught,
But old Santa wouldn't like me to pout.

The old Christmas songs on the radio
Make me cry even when I'm *not* sad,
Who knows why you cry at Christmas?
If I got any bluer it would just be too bad:
This holiday just isn't shaping up well!
And then they play Elvis' "Blue Christmas!"

Well, things have been better
But they've been worse, too,
And after all, it *is* Christmas
And I know this will soon pass.
Somehow it will all seem good in the long run.
So. In spite of it all, Merry Christmas!

Do You Believe In Christmas?

Do you believe in Christmas?
Do you believe in Christmas Day?
Do you believe in Christmas?
And in what the Scriptures say?
That the Father sent His Son
To be sacrificed that way?
Do you believe He died for you,
Do you believe in Christmas Day

Do you believe He came—
He came to earth on Christmas Day?
Can you believe what pain
He suffers when we don't believe
That He's the Father's only Son
And that He came to die for you?
Do you believe He came that way?
Do you believe in Christmas Day?
Do you believe in Christmas Day?
    Do you believe?

Right Christmas

I'm dreaming of a right Christmas
Not like the ones I've come to know
Where the Spirit's missing
And most folks listen
To all the glitz and hype that flows.

I'm dreaming of a Christ Christmas,
Full of His goodness and His love,
Where the meaning of the season
Is the focus and the reason
The Incarnation of God descended from above.

May your days be merry and bright,
Full of His blessings from above;
Let Him fill you all this year
With His presence and His cheer,
And may future Christmases be right.

Christmas Comes but Once a Year

Oft' repeated the words you hear:
Christmas comes but once a year.
Just a month to encompass all that cheer—
Or two or three or four, for some!

Some just can't get enough of it—
Beginning before Thanksgiving candles are lit
And into the New Year before they quit.
For them, Christmas is the best, bar none.

It really comes but once a day,
A special, magical, reverent day.
A holy night, the people say.

For some that magic lasts all year,
For those of us whose hearts are full
Of all things bright and beautiful.
The memories of Christmas stay so dear.
They've even been known to cause a tear,
That Christmas comes but once a year.

But Christmas comes for everyone.

Post-Holiday Letdown

After Christmas, Thanksgiving or Birthday
Comes the inevitable downward spin;
No matter that you try to stave it off,
It happens—you just can't win.
Maybe it's the frenetic hustle and bustle,
The planning, the plotting, the anticipation
Engendered by a happy coming event,
Or all the purchases and preparation.
Holidays are special occasions
To everyone, if you're truthful;
Youngster or oldster it's still the same,
Even if you're no longer youthful

But after it's over and the holiday's passed,
There's no more planning and everything's done,
It may have been all you wanted it to be
But it's just too much for some.
You can't do anything about it—
The weariness is settling in.
Yes, it's mental, but it's physical, too;
A profound lethargy seems to begin;
So overwhelming are the symptoms
If you didn't know better you'd think you were ill:
The blues, the blahs, whatever you call it,
You think it won't pass—but it will!

This Isn't the End

This isn't the end by any means,
To all that I have to offer.
'Tho all these rhymes and bits of verse
Add nothing to my coffer.

As long as I have life and breath
And can make my fingers manipulate
The computer keys, and my brain
Can rhyme and participate

I still will write my poetry.
I'll write of what my day brings;
There's still a lot of subjects left
And numerous little things.

All those important ideas—to me,
If not so much to you—
May yet be added here.
There could be yet a few.

If not, it must be sufficient
That you know they were created,
If not here on earth, then, somewhere
And they will be better than anticipated!

Printed in the United States
By Bookmasters